A MONTH IN
THE COUNTRY

ALSO IN THIS SERIES:

The Inspector
The Cherry Orchard

A MONTH IN THE COUNTRY

A Comedy in Five Acts

IVAN TURGENEV

Translated from the Russian by
Richard Nelson, Richard Pevear
and Larissa Volokhonsky

THEATRE COMMUNICATIONS GROUP
NEW YORK
2014

A Month in the Country is published by Theatre Communications Group, Inc.,
520 8th Avenue, 24th Floor, New York, NY 10018-4156

The publication of *A Month in the Country*, by Richard Nelson, Richard Pevear and Larissa Volokhonsky, through TCG's Book Program, is made possible in part by the New York State Council on the Arts with the support of Governor Andrew Cuomo and the New York State Legislature.

TCG books are exclusively distributed to the book trade by Consortium Book Sales and Distribution.

LIBRARY OF CONGRESS CATALOGING-IN-PUBLICATION DATA
Turgenev, Ivan Sergeevich, 1818–1883.
[Mesiats v derevne. English]
A month in the country : a comedy in five acts / Ivan Turgenev ; translated from the Russian by Richard Nelson, Richard Pevear and Larissa Volokhonsky.
pages cm.
(TCG Classic Russian Drama series)
Includes bibliographical references and index.
ISBN 978-1-55936-467-6 (paperback)
ISBN 978-1-55936-781-3 (ebook)
I. Nelson, Richard, 1950– translator. II. Pevear, Richard, 1943– translator.
III. Volokhonsky, Larissa, translator. IV. Title.
PG3421.M4N45   2014
891.72'3—dc23   2014044685

Book design and composition by Lisa Govan
Cover design by John Gall
First Edition, December 2014

CONTENTS

INTRODUCTION

In 1844, the twenty-six-year-old Ivan Turgenev wrote the beginnings of a one-act comedy entitled *Two Sisters*, consisting of a brief note "instead of a preface," a list of characters and two scenes, the second broken off in mid-page. The manuscript eventually turned up in Paris and was published almost a century later. Turgenev had been serving in the Russian interior ministry at the time and dabbling in various sorts of literary work—fantasies, lyrics, longer poems, plays—most of it quite unoriginal, as he himself admitted. His models were Pushkin and Gogol among the Russians, Prosper Mérimée and Alfred de Musset among the French. A year earlier he had written his first play, the one-act "Imprudence," a slight comedy set in Spain. The publication of his long poem, *Parasha*, in the same year, had brought him some critical recognition. He had also met the French/Spanish opera singer Pauline Viardot, who performed during winter season in Petersburg, and had fallen in love with her, a relationship that was to last with varying degrees of intimacy for the rest of his life. He also became and remained friends with the singer's husband, Louis

Viardot, twenty years her senior, a journalist, art critic and one-time director of the Théâtre des Italiens in Paris, who acted as Pauline's manager. The two men collaborated on translations from Russian into French, of Turgenev's own works among others, and also went hunting together.

The fragment of the new play was written in June 1844, after the Viardots had gone back to Paris. Like "Imprudence," it was to be a French-style one-act comedy of love, also set in Spain, though, as Turgenev remarked in his preface, a Spanish friend told him the setting could just as well be China. The characters' names are a random mixture, none of them Russian: Fabian, a wealthy noble-man, thirty-five; Valery, Fabian's friend, fifty; Nemorino, a poor student, nineteen; Klara, Fabian's lady-love, twenty-three; Antoni-etta, her sister, seventeen. There are also Klara's mute black ser-vant and her pageboy. The fragment suggests that the plot would turn on the rivalry between Klara and her sharp-tongued young sister over Fabian. The student's role is barely hinted at (Antoni-etta pretends to be indifferent when he is mentioned), and he does not appear in the fragment.

Five years later, while living with the Viardots in Paris and nearby Courtavenel, Turgenev began work on a play he entitled *The Student*, which was a major reworking of the earlier semi-Spanish comedy, now extended to five acts, set in Russia, and with additional characters. He sent the finished play to Petersburg in 1850 for publication in the liberal magazine *The Contemporary*, but the censors did not pass it. It circulated in the Petersburg salons, however, with considerable success. Turgenev made some revisions and resubmitted it to the censors under the title *Two Women*, but it was refused again. The censors insisted not only on cuts in some speeches but on making the heroine, Natalya Petrovna, a widow instead of a married woman, because they thought it improper to portray a possible adulteress on the stage. Turgenev finally agreed to all the changes, and the play was pub-lished in 1855 under its definitive title, *A Month in the Country*.

Turgenev wrote ten plays between 1843 and 1852, several of which were staged, though without much success. During those same years he also began to write the prose fiction on which his reputation now mainly rests. His first published story, "Andrei Kolosov," appeared in the magazine *Notes of the Fatherland* in November 1844. (Curiously, he gave the same name to the hero of *The Student* in its early drafts.) Two years later he began to write the stories that would go into his first major work, *A Hunter's Notes* (or *A Sportsman's Sketches*), published in 1852, and considered by many, including himself, to be his finest contribution to Russian literature. These realistic stories, most of them written in Paris, are set in the deep Russian countryside around Turgenev's estate, Spasskoe, in Orel province. The book met with much praise from both liberal and conservative critics. Then, in 1856, a year after the publication of *A Month in the Country*, he brought out his first novel, *Rudin*. And he never went back to playwriting.

In 1869 Turgenev included a volume of *Scenes and Comedies* in a collected edition of his works, prefacing it with a disclaimer: "Recognizing no dramatic talent in myself, I would not have yielded to the requests of my publishers, who wanted to publish my works with all possible completeness, if I had not thought that my plays, while unsatisfactory on stage, might be of some interest to read . . ." He added an intriguing comment about *A Month in the Country* specifically: "In its original version I set myself quite a complicated psychological task in this comedy, but the censorship of the time, having forced me to throw out the husband and turn his wife into a widow, completely distorted my intention." In the 1869 version, which became canonical, he resurrected the husband, but did not restore the cuts that had been demanded by the censors.

Though Turgenev had advised against it, *A Month in the Country* was finally performed in 1872, but the production drew little attention. Then, in January 1879, Maria Savina, a young actress at the Alexandrinsky Theatre, the imperial theater in Petersburg, decided to stage it again in a benefit performance, with herself in the role of Vera. It was a tremendous success. Turgenev visited Petersburg a month later, eventually persuaded himself to attend a performance, where he received a standing ovation, and promptly fell in love with Savina. He was over sixty; she was twenty-five. This was the last love of his life, expressed mainly in the letters he wrote to her while still in Russia and then from Paris, where he died in 1883. "Rakitin is me," he confessed in one of them. "I always portray myself as the unsuccessful lover . . ."

A Month in the Country permanently entered the Russian repertory after the production at the Alexandrinsky Theatre. In 1909 Stanislavsky staged the play at the Moscow Art Theatre, with himself as Rakitin and Olga Knipper, Chekhov's widow, as Natalya Petrovna. His work on the production was of great importance in the development of his "method." He wanted the stage to be almost bare and the acting to be minimal, almost without gestures, an "inner delineation of character" by means of intonation. The Irish playwright Brian Friel echoed Stanislavsky in a note on his 1992 adaptation of the play: "Turgenev fashioned a new kind of dramatic situation and a new kind of dramatic character where for the first time psychological and poetic elements created a theater of moods where the action resides in internal emotion and secret turmoil and not in external events." This understanding bears out Turgenev's comment about the "complicated psychological task" he set himself in the play. *A Month in the Country* is often called "Chekhovian." In fact, Turgenev's theater not only preceded Chekhov's by some forty years, but differs from it in important ways. On the other hand, it was undoubtedly Stanislavsky's earlier work with Chekhov that led to this landmark production of Turgenev's play.

Turgenev was one of the "men of the Forties," as they came to be known. At the age of nineteen he twice saw Alexander Pushkin from a distance, not long before the poet was killed in a duel. His collection of stories, *A Hunter's Notes*, was praised by Nikolai Gogol. But his contemporaries were the liberal intellectuals who emerged during the last years of the repressive reign of Nicholas I, largely in response to its repression. From 1838 to 1841, Turgenev studied classics and philosophy at the University of Berlin, where he made friends with a group of "Russian Hegelians," among them Mikhail Bakunin, later the chief exponent of Anarchism, who was the model for the hero of his first novel, *Rudin*. In Russia and then in their "self-exile" abroad he made the acquaintance of Alexander Herzen and Vissarion Belinsky, two of the most forceful social critics of their time, opponents of the Russian autarchy and above all of serfdom. When his mother died in 1850, Turgenev returned to Russia to arrange the affairs of the estate at Spasskoe. One of his first acts was to free the household serfs; he also enabled the peasants to buy their freedom at rates very advantageous for them. This was more than a decade before the new emperor, Alexander II, known as the "tsar-liberator," signed the proclamation that finally put an end to serfdom. The stories collected in *A Hunter's Notes* were, among other things, a sharply critical portrayal of the conditions of serfdom and the life of the landed gentry. The book's publication in 1852 cost Turgenev a month in prison and a year in "exile" on his estate. He was not allowed to travel abroad again until 1856.

Two figures came to typify the intellectuals of mid-nineteenth-century Russia: the superfluous man, and the nihilist. Both terms were coined by Turgenev, the first in his novella of 1850, *The Diary of a Superfluous Man*, and the second in his novel *Fathers and Sons*, published in 1862. While Turgenev shared the liberalism of his intellectual contemporaries, who often found themselves "superfluous" in the Russia of Nicholas I, he came to detest the revolutionary and utopian extremism that was embodied by the nihilists, the so-called "new men" of the Sixties, whose first spokesman was the thinker and novelist Nikolai Chernyshevsky. Chernyshevsky's thesis, *The Aesthetic Relations of Art to Reality*, which he defended at the university in 1855, the same year that *A Month in the Country* was published, propounded a purely utilitarian notion of art. Turgenev found his writing physically repulsive; Tolstoy said that it "stinks of bedbugs." A later aristocrat, Vladimir Nabokov, gave us the most pitiless and at the same time moving portrait of Chernyshevsky in the fourth chapter of his novel *The Gift*.

In expanding the sketch of "Two Sisters" into *A Month in the Country*, Turgenev made two important additions to the cast: Mikhail Rakitin and Dr. Shpigelsky. They are the two major speechmakers of the play, and their speeches suffered most from the censors' cuts. In the original version of the last act, Rakitin, who is paying the price for his superfluousness, continued his long speech to the student Belyaev, describing the slavery and humiliation of love, by advising the young man to seize his chance with women, not to lose time, not to worry about fine feelings, because a woman's love is like a spring freshet, rushing with water one day, and dried up the next. The censors considered the passage morally inadmissible. Shpigelsky's speech to Lizaveta Bogdanovna in the fourth act suffered even more. His description of his kowtowing to the gentry was a more detailed and pointed caricature of their gullibility and his own duplicity, and in describing his childhood, he confessed that he was illegitimate, the son of a poor girl, had gone about barefoot and hungry, and nursed an undying hatred of the "benefactor" (one of his mother's noble "friends") who had sent him to Moscow and the university to get him out of the way. That was all removed. As for Belyaev, in the original cast list Turgenev described him as a student in the department of political studies at the university. The censors left only the word "student."

The fact that the first version of *A Month in the Country* was entitled *The Student* suggests that Belyaev was to be the central character of the play. And in a sense he is. But not in the way that Soviet criticism thought. In the Soviet view, the play is built on the conflict between the decadent gentry (Natalya Petrovna, Rakitin, Anna Pavlovna, Bolshintsov) and the new forces, embodied by Belyaev and Vera, with Islaev and Shpigelsky somewhere between the two, the one partly justified by his hard work, the other by his poor origins and class consciousness. Belyaev asks to borrow a magazine from Rakitin, probably an intellectual journal not unlike *The Contemporary*, in which Turgenev published his own work. When Rakitin asks him if he reads poetry or stories, Belyaev says he prefers the critical articles, suggesting the practical turn of mind of the "new men." The social and political situation of Russia at the time is certainly implicit in the play, as is Turgenev's hope for a renewal brought about by fresh young people like Belyaev. But if Rakitin is a superfluous man, Belyaev is hardly a nihilist. His freshness is something other than the promise of social change, something more universally human.

What the Soviet interpretation left out was the question of love. And yet love, the force of love, love in all its permutations, is everywhere in the play, like the wind that Natalya Petrovna suddenly lets into the drawing room in Act One:

> NATALYA: Hello, wind. *(She laughs)* As if he's been waiting for a chance to burst in . . . *(Looking around)* See how he's taken over the whole room . . . There's no driving him out now . . .

Belyaev is in some sense the personification of that wind, a local Eros with his homemade bow and arrow. He is a breath of fresh air, of youth, freedom, disruption, in what Stanislavsky called the "hothouse" life of the old country estate. But he is an unwitting and unwilling Eros. His importance lies less in his own character than in the effect he has on the others. The result of his sudden intrusion is a comedy of the unexpected at every turn and in every tone, a constant balancing of absurdity and true feeling, concealment and confession. The play keeps the lightness and quickness of the older French comedies, their repartee and their soliloquies, but transformed by a realism that was new to the stage. Maintaining that balance was the "complex psychological task" Turgenev set himself as a dramatist.

—*Richard Pevear*

A MONTH IN
THE COUNTRY

CHARACTERS

ARKÁDY SERGÉICH ISLÁEV (Arkásha), a wealthy landowner, thirty-six

NATÁLYA PETRÓVNA (Natásha), his wife, twenty-nine

KÓLYA, their son, ten

VÉRA ALEXÁNDROVNA (Vérochka), their ward, seventeen

ÁNNA SEMYÓNOVNA ISLÁEVA, Islaev's mother, fifty-eight

LIZAVÉTA BOGDÁNOVNA (Líza), her companion, thirty-seven

ADÁM IVÁNOVICH SCHÁAF, a German tutor, forty-five

MIKHÁIL ALEXÁNDROVICH RAKÍTIN (Michel), a friend of the house, thirty

ALEXÉI NIKOLÁEVICH BELYÁEV, a student, Kolya's Russian teacher, twenty-one

AFANÁSY IVÁNOVICH BOLSHINTSÓV, a neighbor, forty-eight

IGNÁTY ILYÍCH SHPIGÉLSKY, a doctor, forty

MATVÉI, a servant, forty

KÁTYA, a maid, twenty

The action takes place on Islaev's estate in the early 1840s. A day passes between Acts One and Two, Two and Three, and Four and Five.

ACT ONE

A drawing room. To the right, a card table and the door to the study; in the middle, the door to the ballroom; to the left, two windows and a round table. Sofas in the corners. At the card table, Anna Semyonovna, Lizaveta Bogdanovna and Schaaf sit playing preference; by the round table sit Natalya Petrovna and Rakitin. Natalya Petrovna is doing embroidery on canvas. Rakitin is holding a book. The clock on the wall shows three.

SCHAAF

Haartz.

ANNA

Again? You'll be the death of us, my dear.

SCHAAF

(Phlegmatically) Eight haartz.

ANNA

(To Lizaveta Bogdanovna) Look at him! Look how he plays!

Lizaveta Bogdanovna smiles.

NATALYA

(To Rakitin) Why did you stop? Read.

RAKITIN

(Slowly raising the book) "*Monte Cristo se redressa haletant . . .*"[1]
Are you interested in this, Natalya Petrovna?

NATALYA

Not at all.

RAKITIN

Then why are we reading it?

NATALYA

I'll tell you why. The other day a lady said to me: "You haven't read
Monte Cristo? Oh, you should—it's enchanting!" I didn't answer
her then, but now I can tell her that I've read it and didn't find it
"enchanting" at all.

RAKITIN

Well, since you already know that . . .

NATALYA

Ah, you're so lazy!

RAKITIN

I'll go on if you like . . . *(Searching for the place where he stopped)*
". . . *se redressa haletant, et . . .*"

NATALYA

(Interrupting him herself) Have you seen Arkady today?

RAKITIN

I ran into him at the dam . . . They're repairing it. He was showing
the workmen what to do, and to show them better he had waded
in up to his knees.

NATALYA

He's too passionate about everything . . . he tries too hard. That's a shortcoming. What do you think?

RAKITIN

I agree with you.

NATALYA

How boring! . . . You always agree with me. Read.

RAKITIN

So you want me to argue with you? . . . Fine.

NATALYA

I want . . . I want! . . . I want *you* to want . . . Read, I'm telling you.

RAKITIN

Yes, ma'am. *(He picks up the book again)*

SCHAAF

Haartz.

ANNA

What? Again? I can't stand it! *(To Natalya Petrovna)* Natasha . . . Natasha . . .

NATALYA

What?

ANNA

Imagine, Schaaf will be the death of us . . . Seven or eight hearts every time.

SCHAAF

Und dis time sefen.

ANNA

Hear that? It's terrible!

NATALYA

Yes . . . terrible.

ANNA

Pass! *(To Natalya Petrovna)* Where's Kolya?

NATALYA

Out walking with his new tutor.

ANNA

Lizaveta Bogdanovna, it's up to you.

RAKITIN

(To Natalya Petrovna) What tutor?

NATALYA

Ah, yes! I forgot to tell you . . . while you were away, we hired a new tutor.

RAKITIN

To replace Dufour?

NATALYA

No . . . He's Russian. The princess is going to send us a Frenchman from Moscow.

RAKITIN

What's he like, this Russian? Old?

NATALYA

No, young . . . Anyway, he's just here for the summer.

RAKITIN

Ah! So he's temporary.

NATALYA

Yes, I guess you could say that. You know what, Rakitin? You love observing people, picking them apart, rummaging around in them . . .

RAKITIN

Good God, what are you . . .

NATALYA

Oh, you do, you do . . . So why don't you turn your mind to him.
I like him. Slender, well-built, bright-eyed, confident . . . You'll see.
Maybe a little awkward . . . that you won't like.

RAKITIN

Natalya Petrovna, you're persecuting me terribly today.

NATALYA

Joking aside, turn your mind to him. He seems to have the makings
of a nice man. But, anyway, God knows!

RAKITIN

You've piqued my curiosity . . .

NATALYA

Have I? *(Pensively)* Read.

RAKITIN

"Se redressa haletant, et . . . "

NATALYA

(Suddenly looking around) Where's Vera? I haven't seen her since
morning. *(With a smile, to Rakitin)* Forget the book . . . I see it's
not our day for reading . . . Better tell me something . . .

RAKITIN

Fine . . . What shall I tell you? . . . You know, I spent a few days with
the Krinitsyns . . . Imagine, our young couple is already bored.

NATALYA

How could you tell?

RAKITIN

Can boredom be hidden? Everything else . . . but not boredom.

NATALYA

(Glancing at him) Everything else?

RAKITIN

(After a brief pause) I think so.

NATALYA

(Lowering her eyes) So what were you doing at the Krinitsyns'?

RAKITIN

Nothing. To be bored with friends is a terrible thing: you're relaxed, you're at ease, you like them, there's nothing to irritate you, and yet you're so bored, and there's a stupid gnawing at your heart, like from hunger.

NATALYA

You must often be bored with your friends.

RAKITIN

As if you don't know what it's like to be with someone you love and yet be sick of him!

NATALYA

(Slowly) Someone you love . . . that's a big word. You love words too much.

RAKITIN

Love words . . . ?

NATALYA

Yes, that's your shortcoming. You know what, Rakitin? You're very intelligent, of course, but . . . *(Pause)* Sometimes when we talk, it's like we're making lace . . . Have you ever seen how they make lace? In stuffy rooms, stuck to their seats . . . Lace is a fine thing, but a drink of cool water on a hot day is much better.

RAKITIN

Natalya Petrovna, today you're . . .

NATALYA

What?

RAKITIN

You're angry with me for some reason.

NATALYA

Oh, subtle people, how imperceptive you are, in spite of all your
subtlety! . . . No, I'm not angry with you.

ANNA

Ah! At last, he's overbid! We've got him! *(To Natalya Petrovna)*
Natasha, our villain has to pay up.

SCHAAF

(Sourly) Ist Lisafet Bogdanovna's fault.

LIZAVETA

(Irritably) Excuse me, sir, but how was I to know Anna Semyonovna
had no hearts?

SCHAAF

Ins futur no partners mit Lisafet Bogdanovna.

ANNA

(To Schaaf) Why is it her fault?

SCHAAF

(In exactly the same voice) Ins futur no partners mit Lisafet Bogdanovna.

LIZAVETA

As if I care! Really! . . .

RAKITIN

The more I look at you today, Natalya Petrovna, the less I recognize your face.

11

NATALYA

(With some curiosity) Really?

RAKITIN

It's true. I find some sort of change in you.

NATALYA

Oh? . . . In that case, do me a favor . . . You know me—try to guess what's changed, what's happened inside me—hm?

RAKITIN

Give me a minute . . .

Kolya suddenly comes running noisily from the ballroom straight to Anna Semyonovna.

KOLYA

Grandma, grandma! Look what I've got! *(Shows her a bow and arrow)* Look!

ANNA

Show me, darling . . . Ah, what a nice bow! Who made it for you?

KOLYA

It was him . . . him . . . *(Points to Belyaev, who has stopped by the door to the ballroom)*

ANNA

Ah! It's very well made . . .

KOLYA

I already shot at a tree, grandma, and hit it two times . . . *(Jumping up and down)*

NATALYA

Show me, Kolya.

KOLYA

(Runs to her, and while Natalya Petrovna examines the bow) Ah, *maman*! You should see how Alexei Nikolaich climbs trees! He wants to teach me. And how to swim. He's going to teach me everything, everything! *(Jumping up and down)*

NATALYA

(To Belyaev) I'm very grateful to you for your attention to Kolya.

KOLYA

(Interrupting her heatedly) I like him very much, *maman*, very much!

NATALYA

(Stroking Kolya's head) I've pampered him a bit . . . Get him to run and jump for me.

Belyaev bows.

KOLYA

Alexei Nikolaich, let's go to the stables and bring Favorite some bread.

BELYAEV

All right, let's go.

ANNA

(To Kolya) Come here, kiss me first . . .

KOLYA

(Running off) Later, grandma, later!

He runs to the ballroom. Belyaev follows him.

ANNA

(Gazing after Kolya) What a sweet child! *(To Schaaf and Lizaveta Bogdanovna)* Isn't he?

13

LIZAVETA

Of course, ma'am.

SCHAAF

(After a pause) I pass.

NATALYA

(With some animation, to Rakitin) Well, how did he seem to you?

RAKITIN

Who?

NATALYA

(After a pause) This . . . Russian tutor.

RAKITIN

Ah, sorry, I forgot . . . I was still thinking about the question you asked me . . .

Natalya Petrovna looks at him with a barely noticeable smile.

His face, though . . . actually . . . Yes, he has a nice face. I like him. Only he seems very shy.

NATALYA

Yes, he does.

RAKITIN

(Looking at her) But still I can't quite figure out . . .

NATALYA

Why don't we help him along a bit, Rakitin? Want to? We'll complete his education. Who better than two staid, reasonable people like us! We're very reasonable, aren't we?

RAKITIN

This young man interests you. If he knew it . . . he'd be flattered.

NATALYA

Oh, not at all, believe me! It's impossible to judge him by what . . . our kind would do in his place. He's not at all like us, Rakitin. That's the trouble: we keep studying ourselves and then imagine we know other people.

RAKITIN

"The soul of another is a dark forest." But what are you hinting at? . . . Why this constant needling?

NATALYA

Who can you needle, if not your friends . . . And you are my friend . . . You know that.

She presses his hand. Rakitin smiles and brightens up.

You're my old friend.

RAKITIN

I'm just afraid . . . you'll have too much of this old friend.

NATALYA

(Laughs) Yes, too much of a good thing.

RAKITIN

Maybe . . . Only that doesn't make it any easier.

NATALYA

Well, well . . . *(Lowering her voice)* As if you don't know . . . *ce que vous êtes pour moi.*[2]

RAKITIN

Natalya Petrovna, you play with me like a cat with a mouse . . . But the mouse is not complaining.

NATALYA

Oh, poor little mouse!

ANNA

You owe me twenty, Adam Ivanych. Aha!

SCHAAF

Ins future no partners mit Lisafet Bogdanovna.

MATVEI

(Enters from the ballroom and announces) Ignaty Ilyich is here.

SHPIGELSKY

(Entering behind him) You don't announce doctors.

Matvei exits.

Greetings, greetings, greetings. *(Goes to Anna Semyonovna to kiss her hand)* Good afternoon, madam. I trust you're winning?

ANNA

Winning, hah! I've barely broken even . . . And thank God for that! It's all this villain. *(Pointing at Schaaf)*

SHPIGELSKY

(To Schaaf) Adam Ivanych, with ladies! How impolite . . . It's not like you.

SCHAAF

(Grumbling through his teeth) Viz ladies, viz ladies . . .

SHPIGELSKY

(Going over to the round table left) Natalya Petrovna. Mikhail Alexandrych.

NATALYA

Doctor. How are you?

SHPIGELSKY

I like that question very much . . . It means you're in good health. How are things with me? A decent doctor is always healthy, unless he just up and dies . . . *(Laughs)*

NATALYA

Sit down. I *am* in good health, actually . . . but I'm out of sorts . . . And that's a kind of ill health.

SHPIGELSKY

(Sitting down by Natalya Petrovna) Let's see about your pulse . . . *(He feels her pulse)* Ah, nerves, nerves . . . You don't walk enough, Natalya Petrovna . . . you don't laugh enough . . . that's what . . . Mikhail Alexandrych, why are you staring? I could always prescribe you some drops.

NATALYA

I have nothing against laughing . . . *(With animation)* Now you, doctor . . . you've got a wicked tongue, I like that about you, and I respect it! . . . Tell me something funny. Mikhail Alexandrych keeps philosophizing today.

SHPIGELSKY

(Glancing furtively at Rakitin) Obviously it's not only the nerves suffering—the bile's also rising a bit . . .

NATALYA

You're doing it, too! Observe me all you want, doctor, but not out loud. We all know you're terribly perceptive . . . You're both very perceptive.

SHPIGELSKY

Yes, ma'am.

NATALYA

Tell us something funny.

SHPIGELSKY

Yes, ma'am. But I haven't even—just like that *(Snaps fingers)* . . . tell
us a story . . . Allow me a pinch of snuff. *(He takes a pinch)*

NATALYA

Such preparations!

SHPIGELSKY

My dear Natalya Petrovna, there's funny and funny. It all depends.
Your neighbor, for instance, Mr. Popopkin: show him your little
finger, like this, and he just falls apart, choking, weeping . . . but
you . . . Well, anyway, I'll give it a try. Do you know Verenitsyn,
Platon Vassilyevich?

NATALYA

I think so, or at least I've heard of him.

SHPIGELSKY

The one with the mad sister. In my opinion, they're both mad, or
else both in their right minds, because there's absolutely no difference between brother and sister, but that's not the point. Fate,
ma'am, there's fate everywhere, and fate in everything. Verenitsyn has a daughter, a greenish little thing, pale little eyes, a red
little nose, yellow little teeth—in short, a very nice girl. She plays
the piano, and she also lisps, so everything's as it should be. She
comes with two hundred souls, plus a hundred and fifty from her
aunt. The aunt's still alive and will live for a long time yet. Mad
people all live a long time—you know, every grief has its good side.
She signed her will, leaving everything to her niece, and the day
before I personally poured cold water over her head, which, by
the way, didn't do any good, because there's no way to cure her.
Well, so Verenitsyn has this daughter, not a bad catch at all. He
began taking her out, suitors started to show up, among others a
certain Perekuzov, a scrawny young man, shy, but well behaved. So,
ma'am, the father liked our Perekuzov, and so did the daughter . . .
Why wait? To the altar, and God bless them! In fact, everything was
going beautifully: Mr. Verenitsyn, Platon Vassilyevich, was already

starting to slap Mr. Perekuzov on the belly, you know, like this, and to pat him on the shoulder, when suddenly, out of the blue, a visiting officer appears—Ardalion Protobekasov! At the marshal's ball he sees Verenitsyn's daughter, dances three polkas with her, probably tells her, rolling up his eyes like this: "Oh, how unhappy I am!"—and my young lady goes completely out of her mind right there. Tears, sighs, moans . . . Perekuzov isn't looked at, Perekuzov isn't spoken to, the mere word "wedding" causes convulsions . . . My God, what a story! Well, Verenitsyn thinks, if it's Protobekasov, it's Protobekasov. He's also got money. They invite Protobekasov, do us the honor, they say . . . Protobekasov does them the honor. Protobekasov comes, hangs around, falls in love, finally offers his hand and heart. And what do you think? Does Miss Verenitsyn joyfully accept at once? Too easy! God help us! Again tears, sighs, fits. The father's at his wit's end. What is it now? What do you want? And what do you think she answers? "I don't know which of them I love, papa, this one or that one." "What?!" "I swear I don't know, and I'd better not marry anybody, but I *am* in love!" Verenitsyn, naturally, goes apoplectic on the spot, the suitors also don't know what to make of it, but she stands her ground. So there, ma'am, see what wonders go on around us!

NATALYA

I don't find anything astonishing about that . . . As if you can't love two people at once?

RAKITIN

So you think . . .

NATALYA

(Slowly) I think . . . though, I don't know . . . maybe it only shows that you don't love either of them.

SHPIGELSKY

(Taking a pinch of snuff and glancing first at Natalya Petrovna, then at Rakitin) I see, I see . . .

NATALYA

(With animation, to Shpigelsky) Your story's very good, but you still haven't made me laugh.

SHPIGELSKY

Well, my dear lady, who can make you laugh now, pray tell? That's not what you need now.

NATALYA

Then what do I need?

SHPIGELSKY

(With false humility) God only knows!

NATALYA

Ah, how boring you are, no better than Rakitin.

SHPIGELSKY

Good heavens, what an honor . . .

Natalya Petrovna makes an impatient gesture.

ANNA

(Getting up) Well, at last . . . *(She sighs)* My feet are asleep.

Lizaveta Bogdanovna and Schaaf also get up.

O-o-oh.

NATALYA

(Gets up and goes to them) How can you sit there so long . . .

Shpigelsky and Rakitin get up.

ANNA

(To Schaaf) That's seventy kopecks from you, my dear.

Schaaf bows drily.

We can't lose all the time. *(To Natalya Petrovna)* You look pale today, Natasha. Are you feeling well? . . . Shpigelsky, is she well?

SHPIGELSKY

(Who is whispering something to Rakitin) Oh, perfectly!

ANNA

All right, then . . . I'll go and rest a bit before dinner . . . I'm worn out. Come, Liza . . . Oh, my feet, my feet . . .

She goes to the ballroom with Lizaveta Bogdanovna. Natalya Petrovna accompanies her to the door. Shpigelsky, Rakitin and Schaaf remain where they are.

SHPIGELSKY

(To Schaaf, holding out his snuffbox) Well, Adam Ivanych, *wie befinden Sie sich?*[3]

SCHAAF

(Taking a pinch, importantly) Qvite vell. And yourzelf?

SHPIGELSKY

Still breathing, thank you. *(In a low voice to Rakitin)* You really don't know what's going on with Natalya Petrovna today?

RAKITIN

No, I don't.

SHPIGELSKY

Well, if *you* don't know . . . *(He turns and goes to meet Natalya Petrovna, who is coming back from the door)* I have a little business with you, Natalya Petrovna.

NATALYA

(Walking to the window) Do you? What is it?

SHPIGELSKY

I must talk with you in private . . .

21

NATALYA

Really . . . You frighten me.

Meanwhile Rakitin takes Schaaf under the arm, walks back and forth with him, and whispers something to him in German. Schaaf laughs and says in a low voice: "Ja, ja, ja wohl, ja wohl, zehr gut."[4]

SHPIGELSKY

(Lowering his voice) As a matter of fact, it doesn't concern just you . . .

NATALYA

(Looking out to the garden) What do you mean to say?

SHPIGELSKY

The thing is this, ma'am. An acquaintance of mine has asked me to find out . . . well . . . your intentions concerning your ward . . . Vera Alexandrovna.

NATALYA

My intentions?

SHPIGELSKY

Well . . . to put it plainly, my acquaintance . . .

NATALYA

He's not asking to marry her, is he?

SHPIGELSKY

Exactly right, ma'am.

NATALYA

Are you joking?

SHPIGELSKY

Not at all, ma'am.

NATALYA

(Laughing) Good heavens, she's still a child! What a strange idea!

SHPIGELSKY

What's strange about it, Natalya Petrovna? My acquaintance . . .

NATALYA

You're such a busybody, Shpigelsky. Who is this acquaintance of yours?

SHPIGELSKY

(Smiling) Excuse me, excuse me, but you haven't said anything definite yet about . . .

NATALYA

Enough, doctor. Vera's still a child. You know it yourself, mister diplomat. *(Turning)* And, look, here she is.

Vera and Kolya come running in from the ballroom.

KOLYA

(Runs to Rakitin) Rakitin, tell them to give me some glue, I need some glue . . .

NATALYA

(To Vera) Where have you been? *(Stroking her cheek)* You're so flushed . . .

VERA

Outside . . .

Shpigelsky bows to her.

Hello, doctor.

RAKITIN

(To Kolya) What's the glue for?

KOLYA

We need it, we need it . . . Alexei Nikolaich is making a kite for us . . . Tell them . . .

RAKITIN

(About to ring) Wait, just a . . .

SCHAAF

Erlauben Sie . . . Meester Koleeah hassn't read his lektsion for tootay . . . *(Takes Kolya's hand) Kommen Sie.*

KOLYA

(Sadly) Morgen, Herr Schaaf, morgen . . .

SCHAAF

(Sharply) Morgen, morgen, nur nicht heute, sagen alle faule Leute . . . *Kommen Sie* . . .[5]

Kolya resists.

NATALYA

(To Vera) Who did you take such a long walk with? I haven't seen you since morning.

VERA

With Alexei Nikolaich . . . with Kolya . . .

NATALYA

Ah! *(Turning)* Kolya, what are you doing?

KOLYA

(Lowering his voice) Mr. Schaaf . . . Mama . . .

RAKITIN

(To Natalya) There they're making a kite, and here they want to give him a lesson.

SCHAAF

(With a sense of dignity) Gnädige Frau . . .[6]

NATALYA

(Sternly, to Kolya) Do as he says, enough running around for today . . .
Go with Mr. Schaaf . . .

SCHAAF

(Leading Kolya to the ballroom) Es ist unerhört![7]

KOLYA

(As he leaves, whispering to Rakitin) Get us the glue . . .

Rakitin nods.

SCHAAF

(Pulling Kolya) Kommen Sie, mein Herr . . .

They go to the ballroom. Rakitin follows.

NATALYA

(To Vera) Sit down . . . you must be tired . . . *(Sits down herself)*

VERA

(Sitting down) Not at all, ma'am.

NATALYA

(Smiling, to Shpigelsky) Doctor, look at her, isn't she tired?

SHPIGELSKY

But it's good for her.

NATALYA

I'm not saying . . . *(To Vera)* So, what have you been up to outside?

VERA

Playing, ma'am; running around. First we watched them dig
the dam. Then Alexei Nikolaich climbed a tree to get a squirrel,
way, way up, and he started shaking the top . . . We all even got
scared . . . The squirrel finally fell and Trésor almost caught it . . .
But it got away.

NATALYA

(Glancing at Shpigelsky with a smile) And then?

VERA

And then Alexei Nikolaich made a bow for Kolya . . . and so quickly . . . and then he snuck up on our cow in the meadow and suddenly jumped on her back . . . the cow got scared and started running and kicking . . . and he was laughing, *(She laughs herself)* and then Alexei Nikolaich wanted to make us a kite, so we came here.

NATALYA

(Pats her cheek) A child, a child, you're a perfect child . . . eh? What do you think, Shpigelsky?

SHPIGELSKY

(Slowly and looking at Natalya Petrovna) I agree with you.

NATALYA

Well, there.

SHPIGELSKY

But that's no hindrance . . . On the contrary . . .

NATALYA

You think so? *(To Vera)* Well, and you were having a good time?

VERA

Yes, ma'am . . . Alexei Nikolaich is so much fun.

NATALYA

Oh, is he? *(After a pause)* Verochka, how old are you?

Vera looks at her with some amazement.

A child . . . a child . . .

Rakitin enters from the ballroom.

SHPIGELSKY

(Bustling) Ah, I forgot . . . your coachman's sick . . . I haven't seen him yet . . .

NATALYA

What has he got?

SHPIGELSKY

A fever. But there's no danger.

NATALYA

(As he leaves) Will you stay for dinner, doctor?

SHPIGELSKY

If I may. *(Exits into the ballroom)*

NATALYA

Mon enfant, vous feriez bien de mettre une autre robe pour le dîner.[8]

Vera gets up.

Come to me . . . *(Kisses her on the forehead)* A child, a child!

Vera kisses her hand and goes to the study.

RAKITIN

(Quietly to Vera, with a wink) I sent Alexei Nikolaich everything he needs.

VERA

(In a low voice) Thank you, Mikhail Alexandrych.

Exits.

RAKITIN

(Goes up to Natalya Petrovna. She gives him her hand. He presses it at once) At last we're alone . . . Natalya Petrovna, tell me, what's the matter?

NATALYA

Never mind, Michel, never mind. And whatever it was, it's gone now. Sit down.

Rakitin sits down beside her.

It can happen to anybody. Clouds drift across the sky. Why are you looking at me like that?

RAKITIN

I'm just looking at you . . . I'm happy.

NATALYA

(Smiles in response) Open the window, Michel. It's so nice out!

Rakitin gets up and opens the window.

Hello, wind. *(She laughs)* As if he's been waiting for a chance to burst in . . . *(Looking around)* See how he's taken over the whole room . . . There's no driving him out now . . .

RAKITIN

You yourself are soft and still now, like evening after a storm.

NATALYA

(Pensively repeating his last words) After a storm . . . Was there a storm?

RAKITIN

(Shaking his head) It was gathering.

NATALYA

Really? *(Looking at him, after a short pause)* You know, Michel, I can't imagine a kinder man than you. It's true.

Rakitin wants to stop her.

No, let me say it. You're indulgent, gentle, constant. You don't change. I owe you a lot.

RAKITIN

Natalya Petrovna, why are you saying this to me precisely now?

NATALYA

I don't know. I'm cheerful, I'm relaxed. Let me chatter away . . .

RAKITIN

(Pressing her hand) You're kind as an angel.

NATALYA

(Laughing) You wouldn't have said that this morning . . . But listen, Michel, you know me, you'll forgive me. Our relationship is so pure, so sincere . . . and yet it's not quite natural. We have the right to look not just Arkady but everybody straight in the eye . . . Yes, but . . . *(She turns pensive)* That's why it sometimes becomes hard for me, and awkward, I get cross, and like a child, I keep wanting to take out my vexation on others, especially on you . . . That preference doesn't make you angry?

RAKITIN

(With animation) On the contrary . . .

NATALYA

It's sometimes fun to torment the one you love . . . love . . . Yes, like Tatyana, I can say: "Why pretend?"[9]

RAKITIN

Natalya Petrovna, you . . .

NATALYA

(Interrupting him) Yes . . . I love you. But do you know what, Rakitin? Do you know what sometimes seems strange to me? I love you . . . and that feeling is so serene, so peaceful . . . It doesn't

excite me . . . it warms me, but . . . *(With animation)* You've never made me cry . . . and yet it seems I should have . . . *(Interrupting herself)* What does it mean?

RAKITIN

(Sadly) Such a question needs no answer.

NATALYA

(Thoughtfully) We've known each other a long time.

RAKITIN

Four years. Yes, we're old friends.

NATALYA

Friends . . . No, you're more than a friend to me . . .

RAKITIN

Natalya Petrovna, don't touch on this question . . . I'm afraid—my happiness may vanish under your hands.

NATALYA

No . . . no . . . no. The whole thing is that you're too kind. You're too indulgent with me . . . You've spoiled me . . . You're too kind, do you hear?

RAKITIN

(With a smile) I hear, ma'am.

NATALYA

(Looking at him) I don't know how you . . . I don't want any other happiness . . . Many women might envy me. *(Gives him both her hands)* Isn't that so?

RAKITIN

I'm in your hands . . . do what you like with me . . .

Islaev's voice is heard in the ballroom: "So you've sent for him?"

NATALYA

(Quickly getting up) It's him! I can't see him now . . . Good-bye! *(Exits to the study)*

RAKITIN

(Following her with his eyes) What is it? The beginning of the end, or simply the end? *(He pauses briefly)* Or the beginning?

Islaev enters, looking preoccupied, and takes off his hat.

ISLAEV

Hello, Michel.

RAKITIN

We already met today.

ISLAEV

Ah! Sorry . . . I've been running around all day. *(He paces the room)* It's strange. The Russian peasant is very smart, quick-witted, I respect the Russian peasant . . . and yet sometimes you talk to him, explain, explain . . . Seems clear, but it's no use. The Russian peasant hasn't got this . . . this . . .

RAKITIN

You're still fussing over the dam?

ISLAEV

This . . . so to speak . . . this love of work isn't there . . . it just isn't there. He won't let you give him a clear opinion. "Yes, master, yes, master . . ." But what kind of "Yes" is it—he's simply understood nothing. Take the German—what a difference! The Russian has no patience. Though I respect him, for all that . . . But where's Natasha? Do you know?

RAKITIN

She was just here.

ISLAEV

What time is it? It must be time for dinner. I've been on my feet since morning—no end of work. I haven't been to the building site yet. The time just disappears. Terrible! Can't keep up with it all!

Rakitin smiles.

I see you're laughing at me . . . What can I do, brother? To each his own. I'm a plain man, born to be a farmer—and nothing else. There was a time I dreamed of something else; but I was brought up short, brother! Got my fingers burnt—but good! Why hasn't Belyaev come?

RAKITIN

Who is Belyaev?

ISLAEV

Our new tutor, Russian. Still a bit untamed; but he'll get used to us. Got a head on his shoulders . . . I just asked him to check on the building site . . .

Belyaev enters.

Here he is! Well? What's going on there? Most likely nothing—eh?

BELYAEV

No, sir, they're working.

ISLAEV

Have they finished the second frame?

BELYAEV

They've started the third.

ISLAEV

You told them about the beams?

32

BELYAEV

Yes.

ISLAEV

Well—what did they say?

BELYAEV

They said they've never done it any other way.

ISLAEV

Hm. Is the carpenter Ermil there?

BELYAEV

Yes, he is.

ISLAEV

Ah! . . . Well, thank you.

Natalya Petrovna enters.

Ah! Natasha! Hello!

RAKITIN

Why are you greeting everybody twenty times today?

ISLAEV

I told you, I've been running around! By the way, have I shown you my new winnowing machine? Let's go; it's interesting. Imagine—it blows up a storm, a real hurricane. We've got time before dinner . . . Want to?

RAKITIN

All right.

ISLAEV

And you, Natasha, won't you come with us?

NATALYA

What do I know about your winnowing machines! Go by your-selves—just don't get stuck there.

ISLAEV

(Exiting with Rakitin) We'll be right back . . .

Belyaev is about to follow them.

NATALYA

(To Belyaev) Where are you off to, Alexei Nikolaich?

BELYAEV

Me, ma'am? . . . I . . .

NATALYA

However, if you want to go out again . . .

BELYAEV

No, ma'am, I was outside all morning!

NATALYA

Ah! In that case, sit down . . . Sit down here. *(Points to a chair)* We haven't had a proper talk yet, Alexei Nikolaich. We haven't gotten acquainted yet.

Belyaev bows and sits down.

And I wish to get acquainted with you.

BELYAEV

I . . . I'm very flattered, ma'am.

NATALYA

(Smiling) You're afraid of me now, I see that . . . but wait, you'll get to know me, and you'll stop being afraid of me . . . Tell me . . . Tell me, how old are you?

BELYAEV

Twenty-one, ma'am.

NATALYA

Are your parents living?

BELYAEV

My mother is dead. My father's living.

NATALYA

Did your mother pass away long ago?

BELYAEV

Yes, ma'am.

NATALYA

But you remember her?

BELYAEV

Why, yes . . . I do, ma'am.

NATALYA

And your father lives in Moscow?

BELYAEV

No, ma'am, in the country.

NATALYA

Ah! And do you have any brothers . . . sisters?

BELYAEV

One sister.

NATALYA

Do you love her very much?

BELYAEV

Yes, ma'am. She's much younger than me.

NATALYA

What is her name?

BELYAEV

Natalya.

NATALYA

(With animation) Natalya? That's strange. My name is also Natalya . . . *(Stops herself)* And you love her very much?

BELYAEV

Yes, ma'am.

NATALYA

Tell me, how do you find my Kolya?

BELYAEV

He's a very nice boy.

NATALYA

Isn't he? And so affectionate! He's managed to become attached to you already.

BELYAEV

I try to do my best . . . I'm very glad . . .

NATALYA

So you see, Alexei Nikolaich, of course, I wish to make a sensible man of him. I don't know if I'll succeed, but in any case I want him always to remember his childhood with pleasure. Let him grow up free—that's the main thing. I myself was brought up differently, Alexei Nikolaich. My father wasn't a bad man, but he was irritable and strict . . . everyone in the house was afraid of him, beginning with mama. My brother and I used to secretly cross ourselves each time we were summoned to him. Sometimes my father would hug me, but even in his arms, I remember, I'd go stiff. My brother grew up, and maybe you've heard about his break with father . . . I'll never forget that awful day . . . I remained the obedient daughter until father passed away . . . he called me his consolation, his Antigone . . . he went blind in the last years of his life. But his tenderest affection could not erase in me the first impressions of my youth . . . I feared him, the blind old man, and never felt free in his presence . . . The traces of that timidity, of that constant holding back, may not have disappeared entirely to this day . . . I know, at first sight I seem . . . how shall I put it? . . . cold, or something . . . But here I'm telling you about myself, instead of talking to you about Kolya. I only wanted to say that I know from my own experience how good it is for a child to grow up free . . . Now you, I suppose, were not stifled as a child, isn't that so?

BELYAEV

How can I put it, ma'am? . . . Of course, nobody stifled me . . . nobody paid any attention to me.

NATALYA

(Timidly) Didn't your father . . . ?

BELYAEV

He had other things to do, ma'am. He mostly went around to the neighbors . . . on business, ma'am . . . Or not even on business, but . . . He earned his bread through them, you might say. Doing this or that.

NATALYA

Ah! So nobody paid attention to your upbringing?

BELYAEV

Nobody, to tell the truth. Anyway, it must show. I'm all too aware of my shortcomings.

NATALYA

Maybe . . . but then . . . *(Pauses, and goes on with some embarrassment)* Ah, by the way, Alexei Nikolaich, was that you singing in the garden yesterday?

BELYAEV

When, ma'am?

NATALYA

In the evening, by the pond. Was it you?

BELYAEV

It was, ma'am. *(Hastily)* I didn't think . . . the pond's so far away . . .
I didn't think it could be heard from here . . .

NATALYA

Are you apologizing? You have a very pleasant, clear voice, and
you sing so well. Have you studied music?

BELYAEV

No, ma'am. I sing by ear . . . only simple songs.

NATALYA

You sing them beautifully . . . I'll ask you sometime . . . not now,
but when we're better acquainted, when we've become closer . . .
we will become closer, won't we, Alexei Nikolaich? I trust you, my
chattering is proof of it . . .

*She gives him her hand, expecting him to shake it. Belyaev takes it
irresolutely, and after some hesitation, not knowing what to do with
this hand, he kisses it. Natalya Petrovna blushes and pulls her hand
back. At that moment, Shpigelsky enters from the ballroom, stops,
and steps back. Natalya Petrovna quickly gets up, as does Belyaev.*

(With embarrassment) Ah, it's you, doctor . . . Alexei Nikolaich
and I were . . . *(Stops)*

SHPIGELSKY

(Loudly and casually) Just look at what goes on here, Natalya
Petrovna. I come to the servants' quarters, ask for the sick coachman, and—lo and behold!—my patient is sitting at the table stuff-
ing his mouth with pancakes and onion. What good is it being a
doctor with patients like that!

NATALYA

(Forcing a smile) Ah! Really . . .

Belyaev wants to leave.

Alexei Nikolaich, I forgot to tell you . . .

VERA

(Running in from the ballroom) Alexei Nikolaich! Alexei Nikolaich!

She suddenly stops, seeing Natalya Petrovna.

NATALYA

(Somewhat startled) What is it? What do you want?

VERA

(Blushing and looking down, points to Belyaev) Somebody's calling him.

NATALYA

Who?

VERA

Kolya . . . I mean, Kolya was asking about the kite . . .

NATALYA

Ah! *(In a low voice, to Vera)* On n'entre pas comme cela dans une chambre . . . Cela ne convient pas.[10] *(Turning to Shpigelsky)* What time is it, doctor? Your watch is always right . . . It's time for dinner.

SHPIGELSKY

Let me see. *(Takes out his watch)* It's now . . . I'll tell you, it's now— twenty past four.

NATALYA

There, you see. Dinnertime.

She goes to the mirror and straightens her hair. Meanwhile, Vera whispers something to Belyaev. Both laugh. Natalya Petrovna sees them in the mirror. Shpigelsky keeps glancing at her out of the corner of his eye.

BELYAEV

(Laughing, in a low voice) Did she really?

VERA

(Nodding, also in a low voice) Yes, yes, she fell right off.

NATALYA

(With feigned indifference, turning to Vera) What? Who fell off?

VERA

(Embarrassed) It's nothing, ma'am . . . Alexei Nikolaich put up a swing there, so nanny took it into her head . . .

NATALYA

(Without waiting for her to finish, to Shpigelsky) Ah, by the way, Shpigelsky, come here . . . *(She leads him aside and turns again to Vera)* She didn't hurt herself?

VERA

Oh, no, ma'am!

NATALYA

Well . . . but still, Alexei Nikolaich, you shouldn't have . . .

MATVEI

(Enters from the ballroom and announces) Dinner is served.

NATALYA

Ah! But where is Arkady Sergeich? He and Mikhail Alexandrych will be late again.

MATVEI

They're already in the dining room, ma'am.

NATALYA

And mama?

MATVEI

She's in the dining room, too, ma'am.

NATALYA

Ah! Well, come along, then. *(Pointing to Belyaev)* Vera, *allez en avant avec monsieur.*[11]

Matvei exits, Belyaev and Vera follow.

SHPIGELSKY

(To Natalya Petrovna) You wanted to tell me something?

NATALYA

Ah, yes! Right . . . So you see . . . We must talk more about . . . about what you proposed.

SHPIGELSKY

Concerning . . . Vera Alexandrovna?

NATALYA

Yes . . . I'll think it over . . . I'll think it over.

Both exit to the ballroom.
   Curtain.

ACT TWO

A garden. The next day. To right and left, benches under the trees; straight ahead, raspberry bushes. Katya and Matvei enter from the right. Katya is carrying a basket.

MATVEI

So what about it, Katerina Vassilievna? Please tell me, finally, I beg you.

KATYA

Matvei Yegorych, really, I . . .

MATVEI

You know very well how I feel about you, Katerina Vassilievna. Of course, I'm older than you; no arguing about that; but I can still hold my own, there's plenty of juice in me. And you know I'm the quiet sort. What more do you want?

KATYA

Matvei Yegorych, believe me, I appreciate . . . I'm very grateful to you . . . But . . . I think we should wait.

MATVEI

For God's sake, Katerina Vassilievna, what's there to wait for? Let me remind you, that's not what you said before. As for treating you well, I mean, I think I can guarantee that. You'll be treated so well, Katerina Vassilievna, nobody could ask for more. Besides, I'm not a drinker, and I've never had a bad word from my masters.

KATYA

Really, Matvei Yegorych, I don't know what to say . . .

MATVEI

Eh, Katerina Vassilievna, it's only lately you've started . . .

KATYA

(Blushing slightly) Lately? Why lately?

MATVEI

That I don't know . . . only before . . . you acted differently with me before.

KATYA

(Looking off, hastily) Watch it . . . The German's coming.

MATVEI

(Annoyed) Ah, that long-nosed goose! . . . And I've got more to say to you, miss.

Exits right. Katya is about to go into the raspberry bushes. Schaaf enters left with a fishing pole on his shoulder.

SCHAAF

(Following Katya) Vere to? Vere to, Katerin?

KATYA

(Stops) I've been told to pick raspberries, Adam Ivanych.

SCHAAF

Rassperry? . . . rassperry, das ist agreeaple frukt. You like rassperry?

KATYA

Yes, I do.

SCHAAF

Heh, heh! . . . Und me . . . me, too. I like effryting you like. *(Seeing that she wants to leave)* Oh, Katerin, vait a minute.

KATYA

I haven't got time, sir . . . The housekeeper will yell at me.

SCHAAF

Ehh, nefer mind! See, I'm goink, too . . . *(Points to fishing pole)* How do dey say it, fischink, you untershtand, fischink, das ist fish catchen. You like fisch?

KATYA

Yes, sir.

SCHAAF

Eh, heh, heh, und me, too, me, too. And you know vat I'm telling you, Katerin . . . In Cherman dere's a song: *"Cathrinchen, Cathrinchen, wie lieb ich dich so sehr!"* . . . das ist in Russian: "O, Katrinushka, Katrinushka, goot girl, I luff you zo!"

He tries to put his arm around her.

KATYA

Stop it, stop it, shame on you . . . They're coming. *(She escapes into the raspberry bushes)*

SCHAAF

(Assuming a stern look, in a low voice) Das ist dumm . . .

45

Natalya Petrovna enters right, arm in arm with Rakitin.

NATALYA

(To Schaaf) Ah! Adam Ivanych! Going fishing?

SCHAAF

Chust zo, ma'am.

NATALYA

And where is Kolya?

SCHAAF

Mit Lisafet Bogdanovna . . . piano lesson . . .

NATALYA

Ah! *(Looking around)* You're alone?

SCHAAF

Yes, ma'am.

NATALYA

You haven't seen Alexei Nikolaich?

SCHAAF

No, I haffn't.

NATALYA

(After a pause) We'll go with you, Adam Ivanych—do you mind?—to watch you catch fish?

SCHAAF

Fery klad.

RAKITIN

(In a low voice to Natalya) What's got into you?

NATALYA

Let's go, let's go, *beau ténébreux* . . . [12]

46

All three exit right.

KATYA

(Warily poking her head out of the raspberry bushes) Gone . . .
(Comes out, stops briefly and ponders) Ah, that German! . . . *(Sighs
and starts picking raspberries again, singing in a low voice:)*

It's not fire burning, not pitch boiling,
It's my heart that boils and burns . . .

And Matvei Yegorych is right! *(Goes on singing:)*

It's my heart that boils and burns,
Not for papa, not for mama . . .

Such big raspberries! *(Goes on singing:)*

Not for papa, not for mama . . .

What heat! Stifling! *(Goes on singing:)*

Not for papa, not for mama . . .
But for a . . .

*She suddenly looks around, falls silent, and half hides behind a
bush. Belyaev and Verochka enter left. Belyaev is carrying a kite.*

BELYAEV

(Passing by the raspberry bushes, to Katya) Why did you stop, Katya?
(Sings:)

But for a pretty maid it yearns . . .

KATYA

(Blushing) That's not how we sing it.

BELYAEV

How, then?

47

Katya laughs and does not answer.

So you're picking raspberries? Give me one.

KATYA

(Handing him the basket) Take all of them . . .

BELYAEV

Why all? . . . Want some, Vera Alexandrovna? *(Vera takes some from the basket, and so does he)* Well, that's enough now. *(He wants to give the basket back to Katya)*

KATYA

(Pushing his hand away) Take all of them, go on.

BELYAEV

No, thank you, Katya. *(He gives back the basket)* Thank you. *(To Vera)* Let's sit on the bench, Vera Alexandrovna. I have to tie the tail on. *(Pointing to the kite)* You're going to help me.

They both go and sit on a bench. Belyaev gives her the kite to hold.

That's right. Keep it straight. *(He starts tying on the tail)* What's the matter?

VERA

That way I can't see you.

BELYAEV

What do you want to see me for?

VERA

I mean, I want to see how you tie the tail on.

BELYAEV

Well, wait a minute. *(He places the kite so that Vera can see him)* Katya, why aren't you singing? Sing.

48

After a little, Katya starts singing in a low voice.

VERA

Tell me, Alexei Nikolaich, do you sometimes fly kites in Moscow, too?

BELYAEV

There's no time for kites in Moscow! Hold the string . . . like that. Do you think we've got nothing else to do in Moscow?

VERA

What do you do in Moscow?

BELYAEV

What do you mean, what? We study, we listen to the professors.

VERA

What do they teach you?

BELYAEV

Everything.

VERA

You must be a very good student. The best of all.

BELYAEV

No, I'm not very good. Hardly the best! I'm lazy.

VERA

How come you're lazy?

BELYAEV

God knows! I guess I was born that way!

VERA

(After a pause) So, have you got friends in Moscow?

49

BELYAEV

Sure. Nah, this string's not strong enough.

VERA

And you like them?

BELYAEV

What else! . . . Don't you like your friends?

VERA

Friends . . . I have no friends.

BELYAEV

I mean, your girlfriends.

VERA

(Slowly) Yes.

BELYAEV

So you do have girlfriends? . . .

VERA

Yes . . . only, I don't know why . . . I haven't thought much about them for a while now . . . I haven't even written back to Liza Moshnina, and she begged me to in her letter.

BELYAEV

And how can you say you have no men friends . . . what about me?

VERA

(With a smile) Well, you . . . That's different. *(After a pause)* Alexei Nikolaich!

BELYAEV

What?

VERA

Do you write poetry?

BELYAEV

No. Why?

VERA

Just asking. *(After a pause)* A girl in our boarding school wrote poems.

BELYAEV

(Tightening a knot with his teeth) Really! Good ones?

VERA

I don't know. She'd read them to us and we'd cry.

BELYAEV

Why did you cry?

VERA

From pity. We pitied her so much!

BELYAEV

The school was in Moscow?

VERA

Yes. With Madame Bolus. Natalya Petrovna took me from there last year.

BELYAEV

Do you love Natalya Petrovna?

VERA

Yes. She's so kind. I love her very much.

BELYAEV

(With a little smile) And I'll bet you're also afraid of her?

VERA

(Also with a little smile) A little.

BELYAEV

(After a pause) Who sent you to that school?

VERA

Natalya Petrovna's late mother. I grew up in her home. I'm an orphan.

BELYAEV

(Dropping his hands) An orphan? And you don't remember either your father or your mother?

VERA

No.

BELYAEV

My mother died, too. We're both orphans. What can you do? But anyhow we shouldn't be sad.

VERA

They say orphans are drawn to each other.

BELYAEV

(Looking into her eyes) Really? And what do you think?

VERA

(Also looking into his eyes, smiling) I think they are.

BELYAEV

(Laughs and goes back to his kite) I'm trying to think how long I've been here.

VERA

Today's the twenty-eighth day.

BELYAEV

What a memory! Well, the kite's done. Look at that tail! We should go and get Kolya.

KATYA

(Coming up to them with the basket) Would you like some more raspberries?

BELYAEV

No, thank you, Katya.

Katya silently steps away.

VERA

Kolya's with Lizaveta Bogdanovna.

BELYAEV

Who would keep a child indoors in such weather!

VERA

Lizaveta Bogdanovna would only be in our way . . .

BELYAEV

I'm not talking about her . . .

VERA

(Hastily) Without her, Kolya couldn't come with us . . . By the way, she praised you a lot yesterday.

BELYAEV

Really?

VERA

Don't you like her?

BELYAEV

Her! She can sniff her snuff and good luck to her! . . . Why are you sighing?

VERA

(After a pause) I just am. How clear the sky is!

BELYAEV

So that's what you're sighing about? *(Silence)* Maybe you're bored?

VERA

Me, bored? No! Sometimes I don't know why I sigh . . . I'm not bored at all. On the contrary . . . *(After a pause)* I don't know . . . I must be a little unwell. Yesterday I went upstairs to get a book—and all of a sudden, on the stairs, imagine, I just sat down on a step and burst into tears . . . God knows why. And for the longest time the tears kept welling up . . . What does it mean? And yet I feel fine . . .

BELYAEV

That's from growing up. You're growing up. It happens. That's why your eyes seemed swollen yesterday.

VERA

You noticed?

BELYAEV

Sure!

VERA

You notice everything.

BELYAEV

Well, no . . . not everything.

VERA

(Pensively) Alexei Nikolaich . . .

BELYAEV

What?

VERA

(After a pause) What was it I wanted to ask you? Really, I've forgotten what I wanted to ask.

BELYAEV

Are you so absentminded?

VERA

No . . . but . . . ah, yes! Here's what I wanted to ask. Didn't you tell me you have a sister?

BELYAEV

Yes.

VERA

Do I look like her?

BELYAEV

Oh, no. You're much prettier.

VERA

How can that be! Your sister . . . I wish I were in her place.

BELYAEV

What? You wish you were in our poor little house now?

VERA

That's not what I meant . . . Is your house really so small?

BELYAEV

Very small . . . Nothing like here.

VERA

But what's the use of so many rooms?

BELYAEV

What's the use? One day you'll find out what the rooms are for.

VERA

One day . . . When?

BELYAEV

When you become mistress of your own house.

VERA

(Pensively) You think so?

BELYAEV

You'll see. *(After a pause)* So, then, Vera Alexandrovna, shall I go and get Kolya?

VERA

Why don't you call me Verochka?

BELYAEV

And could you call me Alexei? . . .

VERA

Why couldn't I . . . *(She suddenly gives a start)* Ah!

BELYAEV

What is it?

VERA

(In a low voice) Natalya Petrovna's coming.

BELYAEV

(Also in a low voice) Where?

VERA

(Nodding in that direction) There—on the path, with Mikhail Alexandrych.

BELYAEV

(Getting up) Let's see about Kolya . . . He must be done with his lesson.

VERA

Yes, let's . . . I'm afraid she'll scold me . . .

*They get up and quickly exit left. Katya hides in the raspberry bushes
again. Natalya Petrovna and Rakitin enter right.*

NATALYA

(Stopping) Wasn't that Mr. Belyaev going off with Verochka?

RAKITIN

Yes, it was . . .

NATALYA

They seem to be running away from us.

RAKITIN

Maybe so.

NATALYA

(After a pause) Anyway I don't think Verochka should . . . like that,
alone with a young man, in the garden . . . Of course, she's a child;
but even so it's improper . . . I'll tell her.

RAKITIN

How old is she?

NATALYA

Seventeen! She's already seventeen . . . It's hot today. I'm tired.
Let's sit down.

They sit on the bench that Vera and Belyaev were sitting on.

Has Shpigelsky gone?

RAKITIN

Yes.

NATALYA

Too bad you didn't keep him here. I don't know why the man ever
thought of becoming a country doctor . . . He's very amusing. He
makes me laugh.

RAKITIN

And I was thinking you weren't in the mood to laugh today.

NATALYA

Why did you think that?

RAKITIN

I just did!

NATALYA

Because I don't like talking about feelings today? True! I warn you, absolutely nothing can touch me today. But that doesn't keep me from laughing. On the contrary. Besides, I had to talk with Shpigelsky.

RAKITIN

May I ask about what?

NATALYA

No, you may not. As it is, you know everything I think, everything I do . . . It's boring.

RAKITIN

I beg your pardon . . . I didn't mean . . .

NATALYA

I feel like concealing at least something from you.

RAKITIN

Good God! You make it sound as if I know everything . . .

NATALYA

(Interrupting him) Don't you?

RAKITIN

You're just laughing at me.

NATALYA

So you insist that you don't know everything that goes on inside me? In that case, "congratulations." A man watches me from morning till night . . .

RAKITIN

What's that, a reproach?

NATALYA

A reproach? *(After a pause)* No, I see now: you're not very perceptive.

RAKITIN

Perhaps not . . . But since I do watch you from morning till night, may I make one small observation . . . ?

NATALYA

About me? Please do.

RAKITIN

You won't be angry with me?

NATALYA

Oh, no! I'd like to be, but no.

RAKITIN

Lately, Natalya Petrovna, you've been troubled all the time, troubled by something you can't help, something inside you. It's as if you're struggling with yourself, as if you're bewildered. I hadn't noticed it before I went to the Krinitsyns'. It's a recent thing.

Natalya Petrovna traces lines in front of her with her parasol.

You sometimes sigh so deeply . . . the way someone tired sighs, someone very tired, who can't get any rest.

NATALYA

And what do you conclude from that, mister observer?

RAKITIN

Nothing . . . But it worries me.

NATALYA

I humbly thank you for your concern.

RAKITIN

And besides . . .

NATALYA

(With some impatience) Please let's change the subject.

Silence.

RAKITIN

Do you plan to go anywhere today?

NATALYA

No.

RAKITIN

Why not? The weather's nice.

NATALYA

Lazy.

Silence.

Tell me . . . do you know Bolshintsov?

RAKITIN

Our neighbor, Afanasy Ivanych?

NATALYA

Yes.

RAKITIN

What a question! No more than two days ago, he and I were playing cards in your house.

NATALYA

What sort of man is he—that's what I want to know.

RAKITIN

Bolshintsov?

NATALYA

Yes, yes, Bolshintsov.

RAKITIN

Well, I must say, that's the last thing I expected!

NATALYA

(Impatiently) What didn't you expect?

RAKITIN

That you'd ever start asking about Bolshintsov! A stupid, fat, tiresome man—though I can't say anything really bad about him.

NATALYA

He's not as stupid and tiresome as you think.

RAKITIN

Perhaps not. I admit I haven't studied the gentleman that closely.

NATALYA

(Ironically) You haven't observed him?

RAKITIN

(With a forced smile) And what makes you ask . . .

NATALYA

I just . . .

Again silence.

RAKITIN

Look, Natalya Petrovna, how beautiful that deep green oak is against the deep blue sky. It's all drowned in the rays of the sun, and what mighty colors . . . There's so much indestructible life and strength in it, especially compared with that young birch . . . It seems about to dissolve in radiance; its little leaves shine with some liquid glitter, as if they're melting, and yet it, too, is beautiful . . .

NATALYA

You know what, Rakitin? I noticed it long ago . . . You have a very fine feeling for the so-called beauties of nature, and you speak of them very elegantly, very intelligently . . . so elegantly, so intelligently, that I imagine nature must be unspeakably grateful to you for your refined and fortunate phrases. You chase after her like a perfume-drenched marquis on little red heels after a pretty peasant girl . . . Only here's the trouble: it sometimes seems to me that she couldn't possibly understand or appreciate your fine observations, any more than a peasant girl could understand the courtly courtesy of a marquis. Nature is much simpler, even cruder, than you suppose, because, thank God, she's healthy . . . Birches don't melt and swoon like nervous ladies.

RAKITIN

Quelle tirade![13] Nature is healthy . . . that is, in other words, I am a sickly creature.

NATALYA

You're not the only sickly creature. We're both none too healthy.

RAKITIN

Oh, I know that way of making the most unpleasant things sound inoffensive . . . For instance, instead of telling him to his face: "You, brother, are stupid," you need only say with a good-natured smile: "We're both of us stupid, you and I."

NATALYA

So you're offended? What nonsense! I only wanted to say that you and I are both . . . you don't like the word "sickly" . . . that we're both old, very old.

RAKITIN

Why old? I don't think of myself as old.

NATALYA

Well, anyway, listen: you and I are sitting here now . . . and maybe a quarter of an hour ago, on this same bench, sat . . . two really young creatures.

RAKITIN

Belyaev and Verochka? Of course, they're younger than us . . . there's a few years' difference between us, that's all . . . That doesn't make us old.

NATALYA

The difference between us isn't only in years.

RAKITIN

Ah! I understand . . . You envy their . . . naïveté, their freshness, innocence . . . in short, their stupidity . . .

NATALYA

You think so? Ah, so you think they're stupid? I see, for you everybody's stupid today. No, you don't understand me. And besides . . . stupid! There's nothing wrong with that! What's so good about intelligence, if it's not amusing? . . . There's nothing more tiresome than humorless intelligence.

RAKITIN

Hm. Why don't you just say it without beating around the bush? I don't amuse you—that's what you want to say . . . Why blame intelligence in general for my sins?

63

NATALYA

You've got it all wrong . . .

Katya emerges from the raspberry bushes.

So you're picking raspberries, Katya?

KATYA

That's right, ma'am.

NATALYA

Show me . . .

Katya goes up to her.

Nice raspberries! So red . . . and your cheeks are redder still.

Katya smiles and looks down.

Well, you can go.

Katya exits.

RAKITIN

There's another young creature to your taste.

NATALYA

Right. *(Stands up)*

RAKITIN

Where are you going?

NATALYA

In the first place, I want to see what Verochka is up to . . . It's time she went in . . . and in the second place, I must say, I'm not too pleased with our conversation. Let's drop our discussion of nature and youth for a while.

RAKITIN

Maybe you'd prefer to walk alone?

NATALYA

To tell you the truth, I would. We'll see each other soon . . . Anyway, we part friends?

She offers him her hand.

RAKITIN

(Standing up) What else!

He presses her hand.

NATALYA

Good-bye.

She opens her parasol and exits left.

RAKITIN

(Pacing back and forth for a while) What's the matter with her? *(After a pause)* Just a whim! A whim? I've never noticed it in her before. On the contrary, I don't know a more levelheaded woman. What's the reason for it? . . . *(He paces again and suddenly stops)* Ah, how ridiculous they are, people with only one thought in their head, one purpose, one occupation in life . . . Like me, for instance. What she said is true: you observe little trifles from morning till night, and turn into a trifle yourself . . . It's all true. But I can't live without her. When I'm with her, I'm more than happy—"happy" doesn't begin to describe it. I belong to her completely. For me to part with her would be tantamount to parting with life. It's no exaggeration. What's the matter with her? This anguish, this involuntary sarcasm—what do they mean? Is she beginning to be tired of me? Hm. *(Sits down)* I've never deceived myself. I know very well *how* she loves me. But I hoped that in time this comfortable feeling . . . I hoped! Do I have the right, do I dare hope? I admit my

position is quite ridiculous . . . almost contemptible. *(Pause)* Well, why such words? She's an honest woman, and I'm no seducer. *(With a bitter smile)* Unfortunately. *(Quickly standing up)* Well, enough! Get all this nonsense out of your head! *(Pacing slowly)* What a beautiful day today! *(Pause)* How skillfully she skewered me . . . My "refined and fortunate phrases" . . . She's very intelligent, especially when she's out of sorts. And what's this sudden worship of simplicity and innocence? . . . This Russian tutor . . . She talks about him a lot. I must say I see nothing special in him. Just a student, like all students. Can it be that she . . . Impossible! She's out of sorts . . . she doesn't know what she wants herself, so she kicks me. Children do hit their nannies . . . What a flattering comparison! But there's no need for me to get into it. When this fit of anguish passes, she'll be the first to laugh at this lanky fledgling, this fresh youth . . . Your explanation's not bad, Mikhail Alexandrych, my friend, but is it right? God only knows! We'll see. This wouldn't be the first time, my dear fellow, that after a lot of fussing with yourself, you suddenly stop trying to figure things out, fold your arms, and humbly wait for whatever comes. And meanwhile, admit that you yourself feel rather awkward and bitter . . . That's become your trade . . . *(He looks around)* Ah! here he is himself, our artless youth . . . Just in time . . . I've yet to have a proper talk with him. Let's see what kind of man he is.

Belyaev enters left.

Alexei Nikolaich! So you, too, are out for some fresh air?

BELYAEV

Yes, sir.

RAKITIN

To tell the truth, the air's not all that fresh today. It's terribly hot, but here, under these lindens, in the shade, it's tolerable enough. *(Pause)* Have you seen Natalya Petrovna?

BELYAEV

I met her just now . . . She and Vera Alexandrovna have gone in.

RAKITIN

Wasn't it you and Vera Alexandrovna I saw here about half an hour ago?

BELYAEV

Yes, sir . . . We were taking a stroll.

RAKITIN

Ah! *(Takes him under the arm)* Well, how do you like life in the country?

BELYAEV

I like the country. There's only one trouble: the hunting's no good here.

RAKITIN

So you're a hunter?

BELYAEV

Yes, sir . . . And you?

RAKITIN

Me? No. To be honest, I'm a poor shot. I'm too lazy.

BELYAEV

I'm lazy, too . . . except about taking walks.

RAKITIN

Ah! And what about reading?

BELYAEV

No, I like reading. I get tired of studying for a long time, especially the same subject.

RAKITIN

(Smiling) Well, and talking with the ladies, for instance?

BELYAEV

Eh! You're laughing at me . . . It's more like I'm afraid of the ladies.

RAKITIN

(Slightly embarrassed) What makes you think . . . why on earth should I laugh at you?

BELYAEV

I just . . . never mind! *(Pause)* Tell me, where can I get gunpowder around here?

RAKITIN

In town, I think. It's sold there under the name of poppy seed. Do you need good stuff?

BELYAEV

No, any kind. It's not for shooting, it's for fireworks.

RAKITIN

So you know how to . . .

BELYAEV

Yes. I've already picked a spot—across the pond. I've heard it's Natalya Petrovna's birthday in a week, so it will work out nicely.

RAKITIN

Natalya Petrovna will be very pleased by such attention from you . . . She likes you, Alexei Nikolaich, let me tell you.

BELYAEV

That's very flattering . . . Ah, by the way, Mikhail Alexandrych, it seems you get a magazine. Could you let me read it?

RAKITIN

If you like, I'll be glad to . . . There's some good poetry in it.

BELYAEV

I'm not a poetry lover.

RAKITIN

Why is that?

BELYAEV

I'm just not. Humorous verse seems forced to me, and besides there's not much of it; and sentimental verse . . . I don't know . . . I somehow don't believe it.

RAKITIN

You prefer stories?

BELYAEV

Yes, sir, I like good stories . . . but critical articles—that's what really gets to me.

RAKITIN

Why?

BELYAEV

They're written from the heart . . .

RAKITIN

And you yourself—do you write?

BELYAEV

Oh, no, sir! It's no good writing if God hasn't given you talent. People will just laugh. And besides, here's a surprising thing, please explain this to me: sometimes a man even seems intelligent, but the moment he gets a pen in his hand—all hell breaks loose. No, we've got no business writing—it's good enough if we understand what's written!

RAKITIN

You know what, Alexei Nikolaich? Not many young men have as much common sense as you have.

IVAN TURGENEV

BELYAEV

Thank you for the compliment. *(Pause)* I picked the place across the pond for the fireworks, because I know how to make Roman candles that burn on water . . .

RAKITIN

That must be very beautiful . . . Excuse me, Alexei Nikolaich, but may I ask . . . do you know French?

BELYAEV

No. I translated Paul de Kock's *The Milkmaid of Montfermeil*—maybe you've heard of it—for fifty roubles, but I don't know a word of French.[14] Imagine: I translated *quatre-vingt-dix* as "four-twenty-ten" . . . I needed the money. Too bad. I'd like to know French. It's this damned laziness of mine. I wish I could read George Sand in French. Then there's pronouncing it . . . how am I supposed to deal with that? *Ahn, ohn, ehn, iohn* . . . Disaster!

RAKITIN

Well, that can be helped . . .

BELYAEV

May I ask what time it is?

RAKITIN

(Looks at watch) Half-past one.

BELYAEV

Why is Lizaveta Bogdanovna making Kolya practice so long . . . He must be dying to run around by now.

RAKITIN

(Gently) But it's necessary to study, Alexei Nikolaich . . .

BELYAEV

(With a sigh) You don't need to tell me that, Mikhail Alexandrych—it's not the first time I hear it . . . Of course, not everybody is a loafer like me.

70

RAKITIN

Well, come now . . .

BELYAEV

That I know . . .

RAKITIN

And I, on the contrary, know, and know for certain, that precisely what you consider your shortcoming—this ease of yours, this freedom—is precisely what people like about you.

BELYAEV

Who, for instance?

RAKITIN

Say, Natalya Petrovna.

BELYAEV

Natalya Petrovna? It's with her that I don't feel free, as you put it.

RAKITIN

Ah! Really?

BELYAEV

Yes, and finally, for God's sake, Mikhail Alexandrych, isn't upbringing the main thing in a man? It's easy for you to say . . . I really don't understand you . . . *(He suddenly stops)* What was that? A corncrake? *(Wants to leave)*

RAKITIN

Maybe . . . but where are you going?

BELYAEV

To get my gun . . .

He heads off left, runs into Natalya Petrovna.

NATALYA

(Seeing him, suddenly smiles) Where are you off to, Alexei Nikolaich?

BELYAEV

I'm . . .

RAKITIN

To get his gun . . . He heard a corncrake in the garden . . .

NATALYA

No, please, don't go shooting in the garden . . . Let the poor bird live . . . Besides, you may frighten grandmother.

BELYAEV

Very well, ma'am.

NATALYA

(Laughing) Alexei Nikolaich, shame on you! "Very well, ma'am"— what is this phrase? How can you . . . talk like that? Wait. Mikhail Alexandrych and I are going to help with your education . . . Yes, yes . . . We've already talked about you more than once . . . There's a conspiracy against you, I'm warning you. Will you let me help with your education?

BELYAEV

Good lord . . . I . . .

NATALYA

In the first place—don't be shy, it doesn't suit you at all. Yes, we'll help you along. *(Points to Rakitin)* We're old people—but you are a young man . . . Right? Look how nicely it all works out. You'll busy yourself with Kolya—and I . . . and we . . . with you.

BELYAEV

I shall be very grateful to you.

NATALYA

Well, there. What were you and Mikhail Alexandrych just talking about?

RAKITIN

(Smiling) He told me how he translated a French book—without knowing a word of French.

NATALYA

Ah! Well, then we're also going to teach you French. By the way, what have you done with your kite?

BELYAEV

I took it in. I thought you . . . disapproved . . .

NATALYA

(With some embarrassment) Why did you think that? Because I . . . because I sent Verochka in? No, that's . . . No, you were mistaken. *(With animation)* Anyway, you know what? Kolya must have finished his lesson by now. Let's go and get him, and Verochka, and the kite, and we'll all go to the meadow together—want to?

BELYAEV

I'd be glad to, Natalya Petrovna.

NATALYA

Wonderful. Well, let's go, let's go. *(Offers him her arm)* Oh, do take my arm, what a clumsy one you are! Let's go . . . come on.

They both quickly exit left.

RAKITIN

(Looking after them) So lively . . . so gay . . . I've never seen such a look on her face. And what a sudden change! *(Pause)* Souvent femme varie . . .[15] But I . . . I'm definitely rubbing her the wrong way today. That's obvious. *(Pause)* Well, let's see what happens

73

next. *(Slowly)* Can it be . . . *(Waves his hand)* Impossible! . . . But that smile, that soft, bright, welcoming gaze . . . Ah, God spare me the torments of jealousy, especially senseless jealousy! *(Suddenly looking around)* Well, well, well . . . what wind blows you here?

Shpigelsky and Bolshintsov enter from left. Rakitin goes to meet them.

Greetings, gentlemen . . . I must say, Shpigelsky, I wasn't expecting you today . . .

Shakes their hands.

SHPIGELSKY

Neither was I . . . I never imagined . . . I went to his place *(Pointing to Bolshintsov)*, and he was already sitting in his carriage to come here. So I did an about face and came back with him.

RAKITIN

Welcome, then.

BOLSHINTSOV

In fact, I was going to . . .

SHPIGELSKY

(Deliberately changing the subject) The servants told us everybody was in the garden . . . At least there was nobody in the drawing room . . .

RAKITIN

You didn't run into Natalya Petrovna?

SHPIGELSKY

When?

RAKITIN

Just now.

SHPIGELSKY

No. We didn't come straight from the house. Afanasy Ivanych wanted to see if there were mushrooms in the woods.

BOLSHINTSOV

(With perplexity) I . . .

SHPIGELSKY

Oh, yes, we know you're a great mushroom lover. So Natalya Petrovna has gone to the house? What do you say? Shall we go back, too?

BOLSHINTSOV

All right.

RAKITIN

Yes, she went to the house to invite everybody for a walk . . . It seems they're intending to fly a kite.

SHPIGELSKY

Wonderful. In such weather everybody should go for a walk.

RAKITIN

You can stay here . . . I'll go and tell her you've come.

SHPIGELSKY

Don't go to any trouble . . . Please, Mikhail Alexandrych . . .

RAKITIN

No . . . I have to anyway . . .

SHPIGELSKY

Ah! Well, in that case we won't keep you . . . No formalities . . .

RAKITIN

Good-bye, gentlemen.

75

Exits left.

SHPIGELSKY

Good-bye. *(To Bolshintsov)* Well, Afanasy Ivanych . . .

BOLSHINTSOV

(Interrupting him) What's all this about mushrooms, Ignaty Ilyich . . . I'm astonished—what mushrooms?

SHPIGELSKY

And maybe you think I should have said that my Afanasy Ivanych got cold feet, couldn't face coming straight here, asked to go the long way around?

BOLSHINTSOV

All right . . . but still, mushrooms . . . I don't know, maybe I'm making a mistake . . .

SHPIGELSKY

You probably are, my friend. You'd better think about this. See, we've come here . . . we've done it your way. Watch out! Don't get egg on your face.

BOLSHINTSOV

Yes, Ignaty Ilyich, but you . . . I mean, you did tell me . . . I want to know definitely what answer . . .

SHPIGELSKY

My most esteemed Afanasy Ivanych! It's some ten miles from your village to here; every mile you asked me the same question at least three times . . . Enough's enough! Now listen: only I'm indulging you for the last time. Here's what Natalya Petrovna said to me: "I . . ."

BOLSHINTSOV

(Nodding) Yes.

SHPIGELSKY

(Vexedly) "Yes" . . . "Yes" what? I haven't said anything yet . . . "I know little of Mr. Bolshintsov," she says, "but he seems to be a good man. On the other hand, I haven't the slightest intention of forcing Verochka. So let him visit us, and if he earns . . ."

BOLSHINTSOV

"Earns"? She said "earns"?

SHPIGELSKY

"If he earns her sympathy, Anna Semyonovna and I will not stand in the way . . ."

BOLSHINTSOV

"Will not stand in the way"? She said that? "Will not stand in the way"?

SHPIGELSKY

Yes, yes, yes. What a strange man you are! "Will not stand in the way of their happiness."

BOLSHINTSOV

Hm.

SHPIGELSKY

"Their happiness." Yes. But see what your task is now, Afanasy Ivanych . . . You must now persuade Vera Alexandrovna herself that marriage to you is in fact happiness for her. You must earn her sympathy.

BOLSHINTSOV

(Blinking) Yes, yes, earn . . . exactly. I agree with you.

SHPIGELSKY

You insisted that I bring you here today . . . Well, let's see how you're going to act.

BOLSHINTSOV

Act? Yes, yes, I must act, I must earn, exactly. Only the thing is, Ignaty Ilyich . . . You're my best friend, let me confess to you a weakness of mine: as you say, I wanted you to bring me here today . . .

SHPIGELSKY

Not wanted, but insisted, demanded.

BOLSHINTSOV

Well, yes, let's say . . . I agree with you. But you see: at home I . . . I really . . . at home it seemed I was ready for anything, but now I'm getting scared.

SHPIGELSKY

What are you scared of?

BOLSHINTSOV

(Glancing at him from under his eyebrows) It's risky, sir.

SHPIGELSKY

Wha-a-at?

BOLSHINTSOV

Risky, sir. Very risky. I must confess to you, Ignaty Ilyich, as . . .

SHPIGELSKY

(Interrupting) As your best friend . . . I know, I know . . . Go on.

BOLSHINTSOV

Exactly so, sir, I agree with you. I must confess, Ignaty Ilyich, that I . . . I've had very little to do with ladies, with the female sex in general; I confess to you frankly, Ignaty Ilyich, I simply can't think what can be talked about with an individual of the female sex—and alone at that—especially with a young girl.

SHPIGELSKY

You surprise me. I don't know what can't be talked about with an individual of the female sex, especially a young girl, and especially alone.

BOLSHINTSOV

Well, yes, you . . . But what am I compared to you? That's why I'm counting on you, Ignaty Ilyich. They say in these matters the hardest thing is getting started, so, for starting the conversation, couldn't you slip me some pleasant little phrase, like, for instance, some observation—and I'll go on from there. The rest I'll somehow manage by myself.

SHPIGELSKY

I won't slip you any little phrases, Afanasy Ivanych, because no phrases will be any use to you . . . but I can give you a piece of advice, if you like.

BOLSHINTSOV

I'd very much appreciate it . . . And as for my gratitude . . . You know . . .

SHPIGELSKY

Enough, enough. What, am I bargaining with you?

BOLSHINTSOV

(Lowering his voice) About the little troika, you can rest assured.

SHPIGELSKY

Enough, I said! So you see, Afanasy Ivanych . . . You are without question a wonderful man in all respects . . . *(Bolshintsov bows slightly)* . . . a man of excellent qualities . . .

BOLSHINTSOV

Oh, please!

SHPIGELSKY

Besides, I believe you own three hundred souls?

BOLSHINTSOV

Three hundred and twenty, sir.

SHPIGELSKY

Not mortgaged?

BOLSHINTSOV

I'm not in debt for a single kopeck.

SHPIGELSKY

Well, there. I've already told you you're an excellent man and a top-notch suitor. But then you say yourself you've had little to do with ladies . . .

BOLSHINTSOV

(With a sigh) That's right, sir. It might be said, Ignaty Ilyich, that I've shunned the female sex since childhood.

SHPIGELSKY

(With a sigh) Well, there. That's not a flaw in a husband. On the contrary. But all the same, on certain occasions, for instance, a first declaration of love, it's necessary to be able to say at least something . . . Right?

BOLSHINTSOV

I agree with you completely.

SHPIGELSKY

Otherwise Vera Alexandrovna might think you were just feeling unwell. Besides, your looks, though also acceptable in all respects, offer nothing for the eye, you know, nothing that strikes the eye. And that's called for nowadays.

BOLSHINTSOV

(With a sigh) That's called for nowadays.

SHPIGELSKY

Girls like it, anyway. Well, and then there's your age . . . in short, we can't bring it off by paying compliments. So you can forget about pleasant little phrases. You can't count on them. But you have something much more firm and reliable to count on—namely, your qualities, my esteemed friend, and your three hundred and twenty souls. If I were you, I'd simply tell Vera Alexandrovna . . .

BOLSHINTSOV

Alone?

SHPIGELSKY

Oh, absolutely alone! "Vera Alexandrovna!"

By Bolshintsov's moving lips, it is clear that he is silently repeating every word after Shpigelsky.

"I love you and I ask for your hand. I'm a good man, simple, quiet, and not poor: with me you will be perfectly free; I shall try to please you in everything. Kindly make inquiries about me, and kindly pay me a little more attention than you have up to now—and give me an answer, whichever you like, and whenever you like. I'm ready to wait and will even count it a pleasure."

BOLSHINTSOV

(Repeating the last words aloud) "A pleasure." Right, right, right . . . I agree with you. Only here's the thing, Ignaty Ilyich: it seems you were so good as to use the word "quiet" . . . that is, that I'm a quiet man . . .

SHPIGELSKY

You mean you're not a quiet man?

BOLSHINTSOV

No, I *am*, sir . . . but all the same, it seems to me . . . Will it be appropriate, Ignaty Ilyich? Wouldn't it be better to say, for instance . . .

SHPIGELSKY

For instance?

BOLSHINTSOV

For instance . . . for instance . . . *(Pause)* Though maybe we can just as well say "quiet."

SHPIGELSKY

Eh, Afanasy Ivanych, you listen to me: the simpler you express yourself, the less flowery you speak, the better things will go, believe me. And above all don't insist, don't insist, Afanasy Ivanych. Vera Alexandrovna is still very young. You may frighten her . . . Give her time to think your proposal over. Ah, yes! One more thing . . . I almost forgot: you said I could give you advice . . . Don't speak French. I remember you once called a generous host a "bonzhiban"—you said, "What a bonzhiban he is!" A nice word, of course, but unfortunately it's totally meaningless. You know, I'm none too clever regarding the French dialect myself, but I do know that much. Avoid eloquence, and I guarantee you success. *(Looking around)* By the way, here they are, all coming this way.

Bolshintsov starts to leave.

Where are you going? More mushrooms?

Bolshintsov smiles, blushes, and stays.

Above all, don't be scared!

BOLSHINTSOV

(Hastily) But Vera Alexandrovna doesn't know anything yet?

SHPIGELSKY

Of course not!

BOLSHINTSOV

Anyway, I'm counting on you . . .

He blows his nose. From left enter Natalya Petrovna, Vera, Belyaev, with the kite, and Kolya, followed by Rakitin and Lizaveta Bogdanovna. Natalya Petrovna is in very high spirits.

NATALYA

(To Bolshintsov and Shpigelsky) Greetings, gentlemen. Shpigelsky. I wasn't expecting you today, but I'm always glad to see you. Greetings, Afanasy Ivanych.

Bolshintsov makes his bows in some perplexity.

SHPIGELSKY

(To Natalya Petrovna, pointing to Bolshintsov) This gentleman absolutely insisted on bringing me here . . .

NATALYA

(Laughing) I'm much obliged to him . . . But must you really be forced to visit us?

SHPIGELSKY

Good God! But I . . . only this morning . . . From here . . . Good God! . . .

NATALYA

Ah, he's confused, mister diplomat's confused!

SHPIGELSKY

I'm very pleased, Natalya Petrovna, to see you in such—so far as I can observe—such high spirits.

NATALYA

Ah! You consider it necessary to tell me that . . . Does it really happen to me so rarely?

SHPIGELSKY

Oh, good God, no . . . but . . .

NATALYA

Monsieur le diplomate, you're getting more and more confused.

KOLYA

(Who all the while has been fidgeting nervously around Belyaev and Vera) So, *maman*, when are we going to fly the kite?

NATALYA

Whenever you like . . . Alexei Nikolaich and you, Verochka, let's go to the meadow . . . *(Turning to the rest)* I don't think this can interest you all that much, gentlemen. Lizaveta Bogdanovna and you, Rakitin, I leave you in charge of our good Afanasy Ivanych.

RAKITIN

Why do you think it won't interest us, Natalya Petrovna?

NATALYA

You're intelligent people . . . All this must seem silly to you . . . However, as you like. We're not preventing you from coming with us . . . *(To Belyaev and Verochka)* Let's go.

Natalya, Vera, Belyaev and Kolya exit right.

SHPIGELSKY

(Looking with some surprise at Rakitin and Bolshintsov) Our good Afanasy Ivanych, offer Lizaveta Bogdanovna your arm.

BOLSHINTSOV

(Hastily) With great pleasure . . . *(He takes Lizaveta Bogdanovna under the arm)*

SHPIGELSKY

(To Rakitin) And we'll go together, if you don't mind, Mikhail Alexandrych. *(Takes him under the arm)* Look at them running down the path. Let's go and watch how they fly the kite, even if we *are* intelligent people . . . Afanasy Ivanych, why don't you go first?

BOLSHINTSOV

(To Lizaveta Bogdanovna, as they walk) The weather, today, is very, you might say, pleasant, ma'am.

LIZAVETA

(Mincing) Oh, very!

SHPIGELSKY

(To Rakitin) I need to talk with you, Mikhail Alexandrych . . .

Rakitin suddenly laughs.

What are you . . . ?

RAKITIN

Just . . . never mind . . . I find it funny that we've wound up in the rear guard.

SHPIGELSKY

You know, it's very easy for the advance guard to become the rear guard . . . All it takes is a change of direction.

Exeunt right.
 Curtain.

ACT THREE

The next day. The same set as in the first act. Rakitin and Shpigelsky enter through the door to the ballroom.

SHPIGELSKY

So then, Mikhail Alexandrych, do me a favor—help me.

RAKITIN

But how can I help you, Ignaty Ilyich?

SHPIGELSKY

How? Good God, put yourself in my position, Mikhail Alexandrych. Strictly speaking, this doesn't really concern me. I acted, you could say, more out of a desire to please . . . My kind heart will be my undoing!

RAKITIN

(Laughing) Well, you're still far from undone.

SHPIGELSKY

(Also laughing) That we don't know yet, but I really am in an awkward position. I brought Bolshintsov because Natalya Petrovna wanted it, and informed him of her response with her permission, and now, on the one hand, she scowls at me as if I've done something stupid, and on the other, Bolshintsov won't leave me alone. She avoids him and doesn't speak to me . . .

RAKITIN

Why on earth did you get involved in it, Ignaty Ilyich? Bolshintsov, just between us, is simply stupid.

SHPIGELSKY

I like that: just between us! Thanks for the news! Since when do only intelligent people get married? In other things, maybe, but in marriage a fool's entitled to his share. You say I got myself involved in it . . . I didn't. Here's how it happened: a friend asks me to put in a word for him . . . What, should I refuse him or something? I'm a kind man, I don't know how to refuse . . . I carry out my friend's errand. The answer is, "Thank you very much. Kindly don't trouble yourself anymore . . ." I understand and don't trouble anymore. Then suddenly I'm sought out, encouraged, so to speak . . . I go along. Indignation! Is it my fault?

RAKITIN

Who says it's your fault? . . . Only one thing surprises me: why do you do all this?

SHPIGELSKY

Why . . . why . . . The man won't leave me alone.

RAKITIN

Oh, come on . . .

SHPIGELSKY

Besides, he's an old friend.

RAKITIN

(With a mistrustful smile) Really! Well, that's different.

SHPIGELSKY

(Also smiling) However, I don't want to hedge . . . You're not a man to be deceived. Well, yes . . . he's promised me . . . my outrunner's gone weak in the legs, so he's promised me . . .

RAKITIN

Another outrunner?

SHPIGELSKY

No, in fact—a whole troika.

RAKITIN

You should have said so long ago!

SHPIGELSKY

(With animation) But, please, don't go thinking . . . Not for anything would I have agreed to be a go-between in such matters, it's completely against my nature, *(Rakitin smiles)* if I didn't know Bolshintsov to be a most honorable man . . . However, there's just one thing I want: a decisive answer—yes or no.

RAKITIN

Has it gone that far?

SHPIGELSKY

What are you imagining? . . . We're not talking about marriage, but only about permission to come, to visit . . .

RAKITIN

He can always do that.

SHPIGELSKY

He can, can he! Anybody else, yes . . . but Bolshintsov is a shy man, an innocent soul, straight out of a fairy tale, only he doesn't suck his thumb . . . He hasn't got much confidence in himself, he needs a bit of encouragement. Besides, he has the most honorable intentions.

RAKITIN

Yes, and the horses are good, too.

SHPIGELSKY

The horses are good, too. *(Takes snuff and holds out his snuffbox to Rakitin)* Would you like some?

RAKITIN

No thanks.

SHPIGELSKY

So, so it goes, Mikhail Alexandrych. You see, I don't want to deceive you. Why should I? It's as clear as can be. A man of honest principles, with money, quiet . . . If he's suitable—fine. If not— say so.

RAKITIN

That's all well and good, I suppose; but where do I fit in? I really don't see what I can do.

SHPIGELSKY

Eh, Mikhail Alexandrych! As if we don't know that Natalya Petrovna respects you very much and sometimes even listens to you . . . Really, Mikhail Alexandrych, *(He embraces him from the side)* be a friend, put in a little word . . .

RAKITIN

And you think he'll make Verochka a good husband?

SHPIGELSKY

(Assuming a serious expression) I'm convinced of it. You don't believe it . . . but you'll see. In marriage, you know it yourself,

the main thing is solid character! And who is more solid than Bolshintsov! *(Looks around)* Here comes Natalya Petrovna herself . . . My dear friend, my father, my savior! Two chestnut outrunners and a bay in the shafts! Do something!

RAKITIN

(Smiling) Well, all right, all right . . .

SHPIGELSKY

Look sharp, I'm counting on you . . . *(Runs out)*

RAKITIN

(Following him with his eyes) What a finagler that doctor is! Verochka . . . and Bolshintsov! Though, why not? There are worse marriages. I'll do as he asks, and the rest is none of my business!

He turns. Natalya Petrovna comes out of the study, sees him, and stops.

NATALYA

(Hesitating) It's . . . you . . . I thought you were outside . . .

RAKITIN

You seem displeased . . .

NATALYA

(Interrupting him) Oh, stop it! *(Steps away)* You're alone?

RAKITIN

Shpigelsky just left.

NATALYA

(Scowling slightly) Ah! That provincial Talleyrand[16] . . . What did he talk to you about? Is he still nosing around here?

RAKITIN

That provincial Talleyrand, as you call him, seems to have fallen into disgrace today . . . whereas yesterday . . .

NATALYA

He's funny, he's entertaining, it's true. But he . . . meddles in what's none of his business . . . That's unpleasant. Besides, for all his fawning, he's quite insolent and pushy . . . He's a great cynic.

RAKITIN

(Approaching her) That's not how you spoke of him yesterday . . .

NATALYA

Maybe not. *(Livening up)* So what did he talk about?

RAKITIN

He talked to me . . . about Bolshintsov.

NATALYA

Ah! that stupid man?

RAKITIN

That's also not how you spoke of *him* yesterday.

NATALYA

(With a forced smile) Yesterday is not today.

RAKITIN

For everybody else . . . but obviously not for me.

NATALYA

(Lowering her eyes) How so?

RAKITIN

For me today is the same as yesterday.

NATALYA

(Giving him her hand) I know why you're chiding me, but you're mistaken. Yesterday I wouldn't have admitted that I was wrong . . .

Rakitin wants to stop her.

Don't object . . . I know and you know what I mean to say . . . and today I admit it. I've thought many things over today . . . Believe me, Michel, whatever stupid thoughts I'm filled with, whatever I may say, whatever I may do, I count on no one as I do on you. *(Lowering her voice)* There's no one . . . I love as much as I love you . . . *(A brief pause)* You don't believe me?

RAKITIN

I believe you . . . but you seem sad today . . . What is it?

NATALYA

(Does not listen to him and goes on) It's just that I've become convinced of one thing, Rakitin: we can never answer for ourselves, we can't guarantee anything. We often don't understand our past . . . how can we answer for the future! You can't put the future in chains.

RAKITIN

That's true.

NATALYA

(After a long silence) Listen, I want to be frank with you, maybe I'll upset you a little . . . but I know you'd be even more upset if I kept it a secret. I confess to you, Michel, this young student . . . this Belyaev, has made a very strong impression on me.

RAKITIN

(In a low voice) I knew that.

NATALYA

Ah! You noticed? How long ago?

RAKITIN

Yesterday.

NATALYA

Ah!

RAKITIN

Remember, two days ago, I said there was a change in you . . .
I didn't know then what had caused it. But yesterday, after our
conversation . . . and out in the meadow . . . if you could have
seen yourself! I didn't recognize you. You were like a different per-
son. You laughed, you skipped, you played like a little girl. Your
eyes shone, your cheeks were flushed. You looked at him with
such trusting curiosity, with such joyful attention. And how you
smiled . . . *(Glancing at her)* See, even now your face lights up just
remembering . . . *(He turns away)*

NATALYA

No, Rakitin, for God's sake, don't turn away from me . . . Listen:
why exaggerate? The man infected me with his youth—that's all.
I myself have never been young, Michel, since I was a child . . .
But you know my whole life . . . It all went to my head like wine,
because I'm not used to it, but I know it will all go away as quickly
as it came . . . It's not even worth talking about. *(Pause)* Only don't
turn away from me, don't take your hand away . . . Help me . . .

RAKITIN

(In a low voice) Help you . . . cruel words! *(Loudly)* You yourself
don't know what's happening to you, Natalya Petrovna. You're
convinced it's not worth talking about, and yet you ask for help . . .
You obviously feel you need it!

NATALYA

That is . . . yes . . . I turn to you as a friend . . .

RAKITIN

(Bitterly) Yes, ma'am . . . I hope to justify your trust, Natalya
Petrovna . . . but let me collect myself a little . . .

NATALYA

Collect yourself? Has something . . . bad happened? Has anything
changed?

RAKITIN

(Bitterly) Oh, no! Everything's the same.

NATALYA

What are you thinking, Michel? Can you possibly believe . . .

RAKITIN

I don't believe anything.

NATALYA

Can you despise me so much . . .

RAKITIN

Stop, for God's sake. Better let's talk about Bolshintsov. The doctor's waiting for an answer about Verochka, you know.

NATALYA

(Sadly) You're angry with me.

RAKITIN

Me? Oh, no. But I'm sorry for you.

NATALYA

Really. That's even irritating. Shame on you, Michel . . .

Rakitin is silent. She shrugs her shoulders and goes on with irritation.

You say the doctor's waiting for an answer? Who asked him to interfere . . .

RAKITIN

He assured me that you yourself . . .

NATALYA

(Interrupting him) Maybe so, maybe so . . . Though I don't think I said anything definite to him . . . Besides, I can change my mind. And, anyway, my God, what does it matter? Shpigelsky has all sorts of things going: not all his schemes have to succeed.

95

RAKITIN

He only wants an answer . . .

NATALYA

An answer . . . *(Pause)* Michel, come on, give me your hand . . . why do you look so indifferent, so cold and polite? . . . Am I to blame? Think, am I really to blame? I came to you hoping to hear good advice, I didn't hesitate for a second, I didn't even think of hiding anything from you, while you . . . I see, I shouldn't have been frank with you . . . It would never have entered your head . . . You suspected nothing. You tricked me. And now God only knows what you think.

RAKITIN

Me? For pity's sake!

NATALYA

Give me your hand . . .

He doesn't move; she goes on, slightly offended.

So you really are turning away from me? So much the worse for you! Watch out! But I'm not blaming you . . . *(Bitterly)* You're jealous!

RAKITIN

I have no right to be jealous, Natalya Petrovna . . . Good God, how can you?

NATALYA

(After a pause) Whatever you like. And as for Bolshintsov, I haven't talked it over with Verochka yet.

RAKITIN

I can go and get her right now.

NATALYA

Why now! . . . But whatever you like.

RAKITIN

(Going to the study door) So you're telling me to get her?

NATALYA

Michel, for the last time . . . You just said you were sorry for me . . .
Is this is how you show it? Can you possibly . . .

RAKITIN

(Coldly) Are you telling me to get her?

NATALYA

(With vexation) Yes.

*Rakitin goes to the study. Natalya Petrovna remains motionless for
a while, then sits down, takes a book from the table, opens it, and lets
it fall in her lap.*

This one, too! What is all this? He . . . he, too. And I was still
counting on him. And Arkady? My God! I completely forgot about
him! *(Straightening up)* I see it's time to put a stop to all this . . .

Vera enters from the study.

Yes . . . it's time.

VERA

(Timidly) You asked for me, Natalya Petrovna?

NATALYA

(Quickly turning around) Ah! Verochka! Yes, I asked for you.

VERA

(Going to her) Are you feeling well?

NATALYA

Me? Yes. Why?

VERA

It seemed to me . . .

NATALYA

No, it's nothing. I'm a little hot . . . That's all. Sit down.

Vera sits down.

Listen, Vera—you're not busy with anything right now?

VERA

No, ma'am.

NATALYA

I ask because I must have a talk with you . . . a serious talk. You
see, my dear heart, up to now you've still been a child; but you're
seventeen years old; you're intelligent . . . it's time you thought
about your future. You know I love you like a daughter; my house
will always be your house . . . still, in the eyes of other people you're
an orphan. You're not rich. In time you may get tired of eternally
living in other people's homes. Listen, wouldn't you like to have a
home of your own—all your own?

VERA

(Slowly) I don't understand you, Natalya Petrovna.

NATALYA

(After a pause) Someone has asked me for your hand.

Vera looks at Natalya Petrovna in amazement.

You weren't expecting that. I must admit, it seems a bit strange
to me, too. You're still so young . . . I don't need to tell you that
I haven't the slightest intention of forcing you . . . I think it's too
early for you to get married; I only considered it my duty to inform
you . . .

Vera suddenly covers her face with her hands.

Vera . . . what's this? You're crying? *(Takes her by the hand)* You're shaking all over? You're not afraid of me, are you, Vera?

VERA

(Hollowly) I must do as you tell me, Natalya Petrovna . . .

NATALYA

(Taking Vera's hands from her face) Vera, aren't you ashamed to be crying? Aren't you ashamed to say you must do as I tell you? What do you take me for? I talk to you like a daughter, and you . . .

Vera kisses her hands.

Ah? So you must do as I tell you, miss? Then kindly laugh right now. I order you . . .

Vera smiles through her tears.

There.

Natalya Petrovna puts one arm around her and draws Vera to her.

Vera, my child, treat me as if I were your own mother, or, no, better still, imagine I'm your older sister, and let's talk together about all these wonders . . . Want to?

VERA

All right, ma'am.

NATALYA

Well, listen, then . . . Move closer. There. First of all, since we're saying you're my sister, there's no need for me to persuade you that you're at home here: such pretty eyes are at home everywhere. So it shouldn't even enter your head that you're a burden to anybody in the world and that anybody would want to get rid of you . . . Do you hear? Then one bright day your sister comes to you and says: "Imagine, Vera, someone has asked to marry you . . ." Eh? How will you answer her? That you're still very young, that you're not even thinking about marriage?

VERA

Yes, ma'am.

NATALYA

Don't say "Yes, ma'am" to me. Do you say "Yes, ma'am" to a sister?

VERA

(Smiling) Well, then . . . yes.

NATALYA

Your sister will agree with you, the suitor will be refused, and that's the end of it. But what if the suitor is a good man, with money, if he's prepared to wait, if he asks only for permission to see you now and then, in hopes that in time you'll come to like him?

VERA

And who is this suitor?

NATALYA

Ah, so you're curious! Can't you guess?

VERA

No.

NATALYA

You saw him today.

Vera blushes all over.

True, he's not very good-looking and not very young . . . Bolshintsov.

VERA

Afanasy Ivanych?

NATALYA

Yes . . . Afanasy Ivanych.

VERA

(Looks at Natalya for some time, suddenly begins to laugh, then stops)
You're not joking?

NATALYA

(Smiling) No . . . but I see Bolshintsov has no more business here.
If you heard his name and cried, he might still have hope, but you
burst out laughing. There's nothing left for him but to take himself
back home with Godspeed.

VERA

I'm sorry . . . but I really never expected . . . Isn't he too old to get
married?

NATALYA

What are you thinking? How old is he? He's not even fifty. He's
in his prime.

VERA

Maybe so . . . but what a strange face . . .

NATALYA

Well, no more talk about him. He's dead and buried . . . God be
with him! Anyway, it's understandable: a girl your age can't like
a Bolshintsov . . . You all want to marry for love, not for practical
reasons, isn't that so?

VERA

Yes, Natalya Petrovna, you . . . didn't you marry Arkady Sergeich
for love?

NATALYA

(After a pause) Of course I did. *(Pausing again and squeezing Vera's hand)* Yes, Vera . . . I just called you a girl . . . but the girls are right.

Vera lowers her eyes.

So it's settled. Bolshintsov is dismissed. I must say, I wouldn't find it at all pleasant seeing his puffy old face next to your fresh little face—though, still, he's a very good man. So you see now how wrong you were to be afraid of me? How quickly it all got decided! . . . *(With reproach)* Really, you treated me as if I were just your guardian! You know how I hate that word . . .

VERA

(Embracing her) Forgive me, Natalya Petrovna.

NATALYA

Well, there. You're really not afraid of me?

VERA

No. I love you; I'm not afraid of you.

NATALYA

Thank you. So now we're great friends and won't hide anything from each other. And if I were to ask you: "Verochka, whisper in my ear: do you not want to marry Bolshintsov only because he's much older than you and not a handsome man?"

VERA

Isn't that enough, Natalya Petrovna?

NATALYA

I don't disagree . . . but is there no other reason?

VERA

I don't know him at all . . .

NATALYA

Very true, but you still haven't answered my question.

VERA

There's no other reason.

NATALYA

Really? In that case I advise you to think it over more. I know it's hard to fall in love with Bolshintsov . . . but, as I said, he's a good man. Now, if you had fallen in love with someone else . . . that would be a different matter. But up to now your heart hasn't spoken?

VERA

(Timidly) How's that, ma'am?

NATALYA

You don't love anyone else?

VERA

I love you . . . Kolya . . . I also love Anna Semyonovna.

NATALYA

No, I'm not talking about that kind of love, you don't understand me . . . For instance, of all the young men you may have seen here or on visits, can it be that you don't like any of them?

VERA

No, ma'am . . . there are some I like, but . . .

NATALYA

For instance, I noticed, one evening at the Krinitsyns' you danced three times with that tall officer . . . what's his name?

VERA

With an officer?

NATALYA

Yes, the one with the big mustache.

VERA

Ah, that one! . . . No, I don't like him.

NATALYA

Well, and Shalansky?

VERA

Shalansky's a nice man, but he . . . I don't think he cares about me.

NATALYA

Why's that?

VERA

He . . . he seems more interested in Liza Velskaya.

NATALYA

(Glancing at her) Ah! . . . you noticed that? . . .

Pause.

Well, and Rakitin?

VERA

I like Mikhail Alexandrych very much . . .

NATALYA

Yes, like a brother. And Belyaev, by any chance?

VERA

(Blushing) Alexei Nikolaich? I like Alexei Nikolaich.

NATALYA

(Watching her) Yes, he's a good man. Only he's so shy with everybody . . .

VERA

(Innocently) No, ma'am, he's not shy with me.

NATALYA

Ah!

VERA

He talks to me, ma'am. Maybe he seems that way to you because . . .
he's afraid of you. He hasn't had time to get to know you yet.

NATALYA

How do you know he's afraid of me?

VERA

He told me.

NATALYA

Ah! he told you . . . So he's more open with you than with others?

VERA

I don't know how he is with others, but with me . . . maybe it's
because we're both orphans. Besides . . . in his eyes . . . I'm a child.

NATALYA

You think so? Anyway, I like him very much, too. He must have a
good heart.

VERA

Oh, very good, ma'am! If you only knew . . . everybody in the house
loves him. He's so kind. He talks to everybody, he's ready to help
everybody. Two days ago he carried a beggar woman from the high
road to the hospital in his arms . . . He once picked a flower for
me from such a steep bank, I was so scared I even shut my eyes;
I thought he'd fall and hurt himself . . . but he's so sure-footed! You
could see that yesterday in the meadow.

NATALYA

Yes, that's true.

VERA

Remember, when he ran with the kite, the ditch he jumped over?
It was nothing to him.

IVAN TURGENEV

NATALYA

And he really picked a flower for you from a dangerous place? He obviously likes you.

VERA

(After a pause) And he's always happy ... always in good spirits ...

NATALYA

It's strange, though. Why is it that with me he's ...

VERA

(Interrupting her) I told you, he doesn't know you. But wait, I'll tell him ... I'll tell him that you're nothing to be afraid of—right?—that you're so kind ...

NATALYA

(With forced laughter) Thank you.

VERA

You'll see ... And he listens to me, even though I'm younger than he is.

NATALYA

I didn't know you were such friends with him ... Watch out, though, Vera, be careful. He's a wonderful young man, of course ... but, you know, at your age ... It won't do. People may think ... I already pointed that out to you yesterday—remember?—in the garden?

Vera lowers her eyes.

Then again, I don't want to interfere with your feelings. I trust you both completely ... but all the same ... Don't be angry with me, dear heart, for my preaching ... it's the business of us old folks to pester the young with warnings. But I don't need to say all this. You like him—and nothing more, right?

VERA

(Timidly raising her eyes) He ...

NATALYA

There's that look again! Is that any way to look at a sister? Vera, listen, move closer . . . *(Caressing her)* What if your sister, your real sister, whispered in your ear now: "Verochka, is it true that you're not in love with anyone?" Eh? What would you answer?

Vera looks at Natalya Petrovna irresolutely.

Those pretty eyes want to tell me something . . .

Vera suddenly hides her face on Natalya Petrovna's breast. Natalya Petrovna turns pale and, after a pause, continues.

Are you in love? Tell me, are you in love?

VERA

(Not raising her head) Oh! I don't know what's happening to me . . .

NATALYA

Poor little thing! You're in love . . .

Vera presses herself still harder to Natalya Petrovna's breast.

You're in love . . . and he? Is he, Vera?

VERA

(Still not raising her head) What are you asking me . . . I don't know . . . Maybe . . . I don't know, I don't know . . .

Natalya Petrovna gives a start and remains motionless. Vera raises her head and suddenly notices a change in her expression.

Natalya Petrovna, what's the matter with you?

NATALYA

(Coming to her senses) With me . . . nothing . . . What? . . . nothing.

VERA

You're so pale, Natalya Petrovna . . . What's the matter? Let me ring . . . *(She gets up)*

NATALYA

No, no . . . don't. It's nothing . . . It will pass. There, it's already gone.

VERA

Let me at least get someone . . .

NATALYA

On the contrary . . . I . . . I want to be alone. Leave me. Do you hear? We'll talk later. Go.

VERA

You're not angry with me, Natalya Petrovna?

NATALYA

Me? What for? Not in the least. On the contrary, I thank you for trusting me . . . Only, please, leave me now.

Vera tries to take her hand, but Natalya Petrovna turns away as if not noticing Vera's movement.

VERA

(With tears in her eyes) Natalya Petrovna . . .

NATALYA

Leave me, miss, I beg you.

Vera slowly exits to the study. Natalya Petrovna, alone, remains motionless for a while.

Now it's all clear to me . . . These children love each other . . . *(Pauses and passes her hand over her face)* What then? So much the better . . . God grant them happiness! *(Laughing)* And I . . . What was I thinking? . . . *(Pauses again)* She just blurted it out . . . I must say, I never even suspected . . . I must say, this news stunned me . . . But wait, it's not over yet. My God . . . what am I saying? What's the matter with me? I don't recognize myself. What have I come to? *(Pause)* What am I doing? I want the poor girl to marry . . . an old man! . . . I send the doctor . . . he figures it out, drops hints . . . Arkady, Rakitin . . . But I . . . *(She shudders and suddenly raises her head)* But what is it, then? Am I jealous of Vera? Am I . . . am I in love with him? *(Pause)* So you still doubt it? You're in love, wretched woman! How it happened . . . I don't know. As if I swallowed poison . . . Suddenly everything's broken, scattered, swept away . . . He's afraid of me . . . Everybody's afraid of me. What am I to him? . . . What need does he have for a creature like me? He's young, and she's young. And me! *(Bitterly)* How can he appreciate me? They're both stupid, as Rakitin says . . . Oh! I hate that know-it-all! And Arkady, my trusting, kind Arkady! My God, my God, let me die! *(Gets up)* I must be losing my mind. Why exaggerate! Yes . . . I'm stunned . . . It's amazing, this is the first time . . . I . . . yes! the first time! I'm in love now for the first time! *(Sits down again)* He must go. Yes. And Rakitin, too. It's time I came to my senses. I made one misstep—and here I am! This is what I've come to. What do I like about him? *(Ponders)* So this is it, this terrible feeling . . . Arkady! Yes, I'll escape into his arms, I'll beg him to forgive me, to protect me, to save me. Him . . . and no one else! All others are strangers to me and must remain strangers . . . But isn't . . . isn't there some other way? This girl—she's a child. She could be mistaken. The whole thing is childish . . . Why am I . . . I'll have it out with him myself, I'll ask him . . . *(Reproachfully)* Ah? You still hope? You still want to hope? And what am I hoping for? Dear God, don't make me despise myself!

She lowers her head into her hands. Rakitin enters from the study, pale and alarmed.

RAKITIN

(Goes to Natalya Petrovna) Natalya Petrovna . . . *(She doesn't stir. To himself)* What could have happened between her and Vera? *(Aloud)* Natalya Petrovna . . .

NATALYA

(Raising her head) Who is it? Ah, it's you!

RAKITIN

Vera Alexandrovna told me you're unwell . . . I . . .

NATALYA

(Looking away) I'm quite well . . . What made her think . . .

RAKITIN

No, Natalya Petrovna, you're not well, just look at you.

NATALYA

Oh, maybe so . . . but what is it to you? What do you want? Why have you come?

RAKITIN

(In a moved voice) I'll tell you why I've come. I've come to ask you to forgive me. Half an hour ago I was unspeakably stupid and rude with you . . . Forgive me. You see, Natalya Petrovna, if a man's desires and . . . and hopes are modest, it's hard for him not to feel shaken, if only for a moment, when they're suddenly torn from him. But now I've come to my senses, I understand my position and how wrong I was, and I wish for only one thing—your forgiveness. *(He quietly sits down beside her)* Look at me . . . don't you turn away, too. Before you is your old Rakitin, your friend, a man who asks for nothing except permission to serve you, in your own words, as your support . . . Don't deprive me of your trust, use me, and forget that I once . . . Forget all that might have offended you . . .

NATALYA

(Who has been staring fixedly at the floor all the while) Yes, yes . . . *(Pause)* Oh, I'm sorry, Rakitin, I didn't hear a word you said.

RAKITIN

(Sadly) I said . . . I asked you to forgive me, Natalya Petrovna, I asked if you were willing let me remain your friend.

NATALYA

(Slowly turning to him and putting her hands on his shoulders) Rakitin, tell me, what's the matter with me?

RAKITIN

(After a pause) You're in love.

NATALYA

(Slowly repeating after him) I'm in love . . . But that's crazy, Rakitin. It's impossible. Can it just suddenly . . . You say I'm in love . . . *(Falls silent)*

RAKITIN

Yes, you're in love, poor woman . . . Don't fool yourself.

NATALYA

(Not looking at him) What am I supposed to do now?

RAKITIN

I'm ready to tell you, Natalya Petrovna, if you promise me . . .

NATALYA

(Interrupting him and still not looking at him) You know that this girl, Vera, loves him . . . They're in love with each other.

RAKITIN

Then that's one more reason . . .

NATALYA

(Interrupting him again) I suspected it long ago, but just now she confessed everything . . . just now.

RAKITIN

(In a low voice, as if to himself) Poor woman!

NATALYA

(Passing her hand over her face) Well, anyway . . . it's time I came to my senses. I think you wanted to tell me something . . . For God's sake, Rakitin, advise me what to do.

RAKITIN

I'm ready to advise you, Natalya Petrovna, but only on one condition.

NATALYA

What is it?

RAKITIN

Promise me that you won't doubt my intentions. Say you believe I'm only interested in helping you. That way you'll also help me. Your trust will give me strength, otherwise you'd better allow me to say nothing.

NATALYA

Speak, speak.

RAKITIN

You don't doubt me?

NATALYA

Speak.

RAKITIN

Well, then listen: he must leave.

Natalya Petrovna gazes at him in silence.

Yes, he must leave. I won't speak about . . . your husband, your duty. That's inappropriate, coming from me . . . But these children love each other. You just told me so yourself. Now imagine coming between them . . . It would be the end of you!

NATALYA

He must leave . . . *(Pause)* But you? You'll stay?

RAKITIN

(Embarrassed) Me? . . . Me? . . . *(Pause)* I must leave, too. For the sake of your peace, your happiness, Verochka's happiness, he . . . and I . . . must both leave for good.

NATALYA

Rakitin . . . I reached the point where I . . . I was almost ready to have this poor girl, an orphan, entrusted to me by my mother— married off to a stupid, ridiculous old man! . . . I didn't have the heart, Rakitin; the words froze on my lips, when she burst out laughing at my suggestion . . . but I connived with that doctor, I let him smirk; I put up with his smirking, his compliments, his hints . . . Oh, I feel I'm on the edge of an abyss! Save me!

RAKITIN

You see, I was right, Natalya Petrovna . . . *(She is silent; he hurriedly continues)* He must leave . . . we both must leave . . . There's no other way out.

NATALYA

(Dejectedly) But then what is there to live for?

RAKITIN

My God, can it have come to that . . . You'll get over it, Natalya Petrovna, believe me . . . It will all pass. What is there to live for— really!

NATALYA

Yes, yes, what is there to live for, when you're all abandoning me?

RAKITIN

But . . . your family . . .

Natalya Petrovna lowers her eyes.

Listen, if you like, I can stay a few more days after he leaves . . . so that . . .

NATALYA

(Darkly) Ah! I understand! It's the old routine, it's old friendship you're counting on . . . You hope that I'll come to my senses, that I'll go back to you—right? I understand.

RAKITIN

(Turning red) Natalya Petrovna! Why do you insult me?

NATALYA

(Bitterly) I understand . . . but you're fooling yourself.

RAKITIN

What? After your promises, after I—for you, for you alone, for your happiness, for your position in society . . .

NATALYA

Ah! Since when are you so concerned about that? Why have you never talked to me about that before?

RAKITIN

(Getting up) I'll leave today, Natalya Petrovna, right now, and you'll never see me again . . . *(Makes as if to leave)*

NATALYA

(Holding her arms out to him) Michel, forgive me, I don't know what I'm saying . . . You see what a state I'm in. Forgive me.

RAKITIN

(Quickly goes back to her and takes her hands) Natalya Petrovna . . .

NATALYA

Oh, Michel, I can't tell you how hard it is for me . . . *(Leans on his shoulder and presses a handkerchief to her eyes)* Help me. Without you it *will* be the end of me . . .

Just then the door to the drawing room opens, and Islaev and Anna Semyonovna enter.

ISLAEV

(Loudly) I've always been of the opinion . . .

Stops in amazement at the sight of Rakitin and Natalya Petrovna. Natalya Petrovna looks around and quickly exits. Rakitin stays where he is, extremely embarrassed.

(To Rakitin) What does this mean? What's this scene?

RAKITIN

Just . . . nothing . . . it's . . .

ISLAEV

Is Natalya Petrovna unwell, or something?

RAKITIN

No . . . but . . .

ISLAEV

And why did she suddenly run away? What were you talking about? She seemed to be crying . . . You were comforting her . . . What is it?

RAKITIN

Really, it's nothing.

ANNA

But how can it be nothing, Mikhail Alexandrych? *(Pause)* I'll go and see . . . *(She makes as if to go to the study)*

RAKITIN

(Stopping her) No, please, you'd better leave her alone for now, I beg you.

ISLAEV

What's this all about? Tell me, will you?!

RAKITIN

I swear it's nothing . . . Listen, I promise both of you, I'll explain it all later. I give you my word. But for now, please, if you trust me, don't ask me anything—and don't trouble Natalya Petrovna.

ISLAEV

All right . . . but I'm surprised. This has never happened to Natasha before. It's quite extraordinary.

ANNA

What I'd like to know is—what made Natasha cry? And why did she leave? . . . We're not strangers, are we?

RAKITIN

What are you saying! How can you! But listen—I must tell you, we didn't finish what we were talking about . . . I ask you . . . both . . . leave us alone for a little while.

ISLAEV

Well! So there's some secret between you?

RAKITIN

There is . . . but you'll learn it.

ISLAEV

(Having reflected) Let's go, mama . . . we'll leave them. Let them finish their secret conversation.

ANNA

But . . .

ISLAEV

Let's go, let's go. You heard, he promises to explain everything.

RAKITIN

You needn't worry . . .

ISLAEV

(Coldly) Oh, I'm not worried in the least! *(To Anna Semyonovna)* Let's go.

They both exit.

RAKITIN

(Following them with his eyes, then quickly going to the study door) Natalya Petrovna . . . Natalya Petrovna, come out, I beg you.

NATALYA

(Comes out of the study, very pale) What did they say?

RAKITIN

Nothing, calm yourself . . . They were a bit surprised. Your husband thought you were unwell . . . He saw how upset you were . . . Sit down. You can barely stand . . .

Natalya Petrovna sits down.

I told him . . . I asked him not to trouble you . . . to leave us alone.

NATALYA

And he agreed?

RAKITIN

Yes. I did have to promise him I'd explain everything tomorrow . . . Why did you leave?

NATALYA

(Bitterly) Why! . . . But what are you going to tell him?

RAKITIN

I . . . I'll think up something. That's not the point now . . . We must make use of the time we have. You see, it can't go on like this . . . You're in no condition to bear such anxieties . . . you're too good for that . . . I, too . . . But we won't talk about that. Just be strong, and I . . . Listen, you do agree with me . . .

NATALYA

About what?

RAKITIN

About the necessity of . . . our leaving? You agree? In that case, there's no call for delay. If you'll allow me, I'll talk with Belyaev right now . . . He's a decent man, he'll understand . . .

NATALYA

You want to talk with him? You? But what can you tell him?

RAKITIN

I . . .

NATALYA

(After a pause) Listen, Rakitin, doesn't it seem to you as if we're both mad? . . . I got frightened, I frightened you, and maybe all over nothing.

RAKITIN

How's that?

NATALYA

Really. What are we doing? Not so long ago, everything seemed so calm, so peaceful in this house . . . and suddenly . . . where did it all come from? Really, we've all lost our minds. Come on, enough of this foolishness . . . Let's live like before . . . And you won't explain anything to Arkady; I'll tell him about our silliness myself, and we'll both have a good laugh. I don't need a go-between with my own husband!

RAKITIN

Now you're frightening me, Natalya Petrovna. You smile, and you're pale as death . . . Remember what you told me just fifteen minutes ago . . .

NATALYA

What of it! But, anyway, I see what you're doing . . . You stirred up this storm yourself . . . so that at least you won't go down alone.

RAKITIN

Again, again suspicion, again a reproach, Natalya Petrovna . . . God help you . . . but you're torturing me. Or maybe you regret being so frank?

NATALYA

I don't regret anything.

RAKITIN

Then what are you telling me?

NATALYA

(With animation) Rakitin, if you say so much as one word about me to Belyaev, I'll never forgive you.

RAKITIN

Ah, so that's it! . . . Don't worry, Natalya Petrovna. Not only will I not tell Mr. Belyaev anything, I won't even say good-bye to him when I leave here. I'm not going to force my services on anyone.

NATALYA

(Slightly embarrassed) Maybe you think I've changed my mind about . . . his leaving?

RAKITIN

I don't think anything.

NATALYA

On the contrary, I'm so convinced of the necessity, as you put it, of his leaving, that I'm going to dismiss him myself. *(Pause)* Yes, I'll dismiss him myself.

RAKITIN

You?

NATALYA

Yes, me. And right now. Send him to me, will you?

RAKITIN

What? Right now?

NATALYA

Right now. Will you, Rakitin? You see, I'm calm now. Besides, nobody will interrupt us now. I should take advantage of that . . . I'll be grateful to you. I'm going to question him.

RAKITIN

Good God, he won't tell you anything! He admitted to me himself that he feels awkward around you.

NATALYA

(Suspiciously) Ah! So you've already talked with him about me?

Rakitin shrugs.

Well, forgive me, forgive me, Michel, and send him to me. You'll see, I'll dismiss him, and it will all be over. It will all pass and be forgotten, like a bad dream. Do send him to me. I really need to have a final talk with him. You'll be pleased with me. Do send him.

RAKITIN

(Who has not taken his eyes off her all the while, coldly and sadly) As you like. Your wish shall be fulfilled. *(Goes to the ballroom door)*

NATALYA

(Following him with her eyes) Thank you, Michel.

RAKITIN

(Turning) Oh, spare me your thanks . . . *(Exits quickly to the ballroom)*

NATALYA

(Alone, after a pause) He's a fine man . . . But can it be that I once loved him? *(Gets up)* He's right. The young man must leave. But how to dismiss him! I only want to know if he really likes the girl. Maybe it's all nothing. How could I have become so agitated . . . why all these emotions? Well, there's nothing to be done now. I wish I knew what he'll tell me. But he must leave . . . He must . . . he must. Maybe he won't want to answer me . . . He's afraid of me . . . Well? So much the better. There's no need to say much to him . . . *(Puts her hand to her forehead)* And I've got a headache. Shouldn't I put it off till tomorrow? In fact, I should. I feel like everybody's watching me today . . . What am I saying! No, it's better to get it over with . . . One last effort, and I'm free! . . . Oh, yes, I want so much to be free and at peace!

Belyaev enters from the ballroom.

It's him . . .

BELYAEV

(Going to her) Natalya Petrovna, Mikhail Alexandrych told me you wanted to see me . . .

NATALYA

(With some effort) Yes, right . . . I need to . . . have a talk with you.

BELYAEV

A talk?

NATALYA

(Not looking at him) Yes . . . a talk. *(Pause)* Allow me to tell you, Alexei Nikolaich, that I . . . I'm not pleased with you.

BELYAEV

May I know the reason?

NATALYA

Listen to me . . . I . . . I really don't know how to begin. By the way,
I want you to know that my displeasure does not come from any
neglect . . . of your duties . . . On the contrary, I like the way you
treat Kolya.

BELYAEV

Then what can it be?

NATALYA

(Glancing at him) You needn't worry . . . It's not really your fault.
You're young. You've probably never lived in a strange house. You
couldn't have foreseen . . .

BELYAEV

But, Natalya Petrovna . . .

NATALYA

You want to know what it's all about? I understand your impatience. Well, then, I must tell you that Verochka . . . *(Glancing at
him)* . . . Verochka has confessed everything to me.

BELYAEV

(In amazement) Vera Alexandrovna? What could she have confessed to you? And what have I got to do with it?

NATALYA

So you really don't know what she might have confessed? You
can't guess?

BELYAEV

Me? No.

NATALYA

In that case forgive me. If you really can't guess, I must ask you to
forgive me. I thought . . . I was wrong. But, allow me to tell you,
I don't believe you. I know why you're saying this . . . I respect your
discretion.

BELYAEV

I have no idea what you're referring to, Natalya Petrovna.

NATALYA

Really? So I'm to believe that you haven't noticed the way this child, Vera, feels about you?

BELYAEV

The way she feels about me? I don't even know what to say . . . Good God. It seems to me that with Vera Alexandrovna I've always been the same as . . .

NATALYA

As you've been with everyone, right? *(A brief pause)* Be that as it may, whether you really don't know or are pretending you don't know, the thing is the girl loves you. She confessed it to me herself. Now I ask you, as an honorable man, what do you intend to do?

BELYAEV

(Embarrassed) What do I intend to do?

NATALYA

(Her arms crossed) Yes.

BELYAEV

This is all so unexpected, Natalya Petrovna . . .

NATALYA

(After a pause) Alexei Nikolaich, I see . . . I'm not handling this matter in the right way. You don't understand me. You think I'm angry with you . . . but I . . . I'm just . . . slightly upset. That's only natural. Calm yourself. Let's sit down.

They sit down.

I'll be frank with you, Alexei Nikolaich, and you be at least a little more trusting of me. Really, you needn't be standoffish with me. Vera loves you . . . of course, you're not to blame for that. I'm prepared to assume that you're not to blame for it. But you see, Alexei Nikolaich, she's an orphan, and my ward: I'm responsible for her, for her future, for her happiness. She's still young, and I'm sure that the feeling you inspired in her may soon disappear . . . at her age love doesn't last. But you understand that it was my duty to warn you. It's always dangerous to play with fire . . . and I have no doubt that, now that you know her feeling for you, you will change the way you behave with her, that you will avoid meetings, strolls in the garden . . . Right? I'm counting on you . . . I'd be wary of talking so openly with anyone else.

BELYAEV

Natalya Petrovna, believe me, I can appreciate . . .

NATALYA

I'll say again that I have no doubts about you . . . besides, it will all remain a secret between us.

BELYAEV

I must say, Natalya Petrovna, everything you've told me seems so strange . . . of course, I wouldn't dare to question it, but . . .

NATALYA

Listen, Alexei Nikolaich. Everything I've told you now . . . I've told you assuming that on your part there's nothing . . . *(Interrupts herself)* . . . because otherwise . . . of course, I still know little about you, but I know enough to see no reason for opposing your intentions. You're not rich . . . but you're young, you have a future, and when two people love each other . . . I repeat, I considered it my duty to warn you, as an honorable man, with regard to the consequences of your acquaintance with Vera, but if you . . .

BELYAEV

(Bewildered) I really don't know what you're trying to say, Natalya Petrovna . . .

NATALYA

(Hurriedly) Oh, believe me, I'm not asking you to confess anything. Even without that I . . . I can see by the way you're acting . . . *(Glancing at him)* However, I must tell you, it seemed to Vera that you were not entirely indifferent to her.

BELYAEV

(Is silent, gets up) Natalya Petrovna, I see that I cannot remain in your house.

NATALYA

(Flaring up) You might have waited for me to dismiss you . . . *(Gets up)*

BELYAEV

You were frank with me . . . Allow me to be frank with you as well. I do not love Vera Alexandrovna. At least, I don't love her the way you suppose.

NATALYA

Did I . . . *(Stops)*

BELYAEV

And if Vera Alexandrovna likes me, if it seemed to her that I'm not, as you say, indifferent to her, I don't want to deceive her. I'll tell her the whole truth myself. But after such a talk, you understand, Natalya Petrovna, it will be difficult for me to remain here: my position will be too awkward. I won't start telling you how hard it is to leave your house . . . but there's nothing else I can do . . . I'll always remember you with gratitude . . . Allow me to go now . . . I'll still come and say good-bye to you.

NATALYA

(With feigned indifference) As you wish . . . But, I must say this is not what I was expecting . . . This was not why I wanted to talk

with you . . . I merely wanted to warn you . . . Vera is still a child . . . I may have made too much of it all. I see no need for you to leave. But, as you wish.

BELYAEV

Natalya Petrovna . . . it's really no longer possible for me to stay here.

NATALYA

You obviously find it very easy to part from us!

BELYAEV

No, it's not easy.

NATALYA

I'm not in the habit of keeping people against their will . . . but, I must say, this is all very unpleasant.

BELYAEV

(After some hesitation) Natalya Petrovna . . . I wouldn't want to cause you the slightest unpleasantness . . . I'll stay.

NATALYA

(Suspiciously) Ah! . . . *(Pause)* I didn't expect you to change your mind so quickly . . . I'm grateful to you, but . . . Let me think. Maybe you're right; maybe you do have to go. I'll think, I'll let you know. May I keep things uncertain until this evening?

BELYAEV

I'm willing to wait as long as you like. *(He bows and makes as if to leave)*

NATALYA

Promise me . . .

BELYAEV

(Stopping) What, ma'am?

NATALYA

Didn't you say you wanted to have a talk with Vera ... I'm not sure that would be proper. Anyway, I'll let you know my decision. I'm beginning to think you really may have to go. Good-bye.

Belyaev bows for the second time and exits to the ballroom. Natalya Petrovna follows him with her eyes.

Peace! He doesn't love her ... *(Strolls about the room)* And so, instead of dismissing him, I've kept him. He's staying ... But what am I going to tell Rakitin? What have I done? *(Pause)* And what right did I have to give away this poor girl's love? ... How could I? I wheedled a confession out of her ... a half confession ... and then so mercilessly, so crudely ... *(Covers her face with her hands)* Maybe he was beginning to love her ... What right did I have to trample on that flower in the bud? ... But maybe I didn't trample on it. Maybe he tricked me ... While I was trying to trick him! ... Oh, no! He's much too decent for that ... Not like me! Why was I in such a hurry? I just blurted it all out! *(Sighing)* Well, so what! If only I'd known ... I was so devious, I was so false with him ... And he talked so confidently, so freely ... I bowed to him ... He's a man! I didn't know him yet ... He must leave. If he stays ... I feel I'll finally lose all respect for myself ... He must leave, or I'm lost! I'll write to him before he has time to see Vera ... He must leave!

She quickly exits to the study.
    Curtain.

ACT FOUR

Evening of the same day. A large, empty hall. Bare walls, uneven stone floor; six brick columns with peeling whitewash, three on each side, hold up the ceiling. To the left, two open windows and the door to the garden. To the right, the door to the corridor leading to the main building; straight ahead, the iron door to the storeroom. Next to the first column on the right, a green garden bench; in one corner, several shovels, watering cans and flower pots. Red rays of the sun fall through the windows onto the floor.

KATYA

(Enters through the right door, walks briskly to the window, and for some time looks out to the garden) No, I don't see him. They said he went to the greenhouse. It means he's still there. So I'll wait till he passes by. There's no other way . . . *(Sighs and leans against the window)* He's leaving, they say. *(Sighs again)* What are we going to do without him . . . Poor miss! How she begged me . . . Well, why not be a help? Let her talk with him one last time. Such a warm

day! And it seems to be sprinkling ... *(Looks out the window again and suddenly backs away)* Are they coming here? Yes, they are. Oh, lord ...

She wants to run away, but before she reaches the door to the corridor, Shpigelsky and Lizaveta Bogdanovna enter from the garden. Katya hides behind a column.

SHPIGELSKY
(Shaking rain off his hat) We can wait here till the rain stops. It won't last.

LIZAVETA
Probably not.

SHPIGELSKY
(Looking around) What is this, some kind of storeroom?

LIZAVETA
(Pointing to the iron door) No, the storeroom is there. They say Arkady Sergeich's father had this addition built when he came back from foreign lands.

SHPIGELSKY
Ah! I see what it is. Here we are in Venice, ladies and gentlemen! *(Sits down on the bench)* Let's sit down.

Lizaveta Bogdanovna sits down.

You must admit, Lizaveta Bogdanovna, this shower was untimely. It interrupted our talk at the most sensitive spot.

LIZAVETA
(Lowering her eyes) Ignaty Ilyich ...

SHPIGELSKY
But nothing keeps us from taking it up again ... By the way, you say Anna Semyonovna's out of sorts today?

LIZAVETA

Yes, she is. She even had dinner in her room.

SHPIGELSKY

Well, now! That's really serious!

LIZAVETA

This morning she found Natalya Petrovna in tears ... with Mikhail Alexandrych ... Of course, he's like one of the family, but still ... Anyway, Mikhail Alexandrych promised to explain everything.

SHPIGELSKY

Oh, she needn't worry. In my opinion, Mikhail Alexandrych has never been a dangerous man, and now less than ever.

LIZAVETA

What do you mean?

SHPIGELSKY

Just that. He's got a facile tongue. Some break out in a rash, the smart ones break out in babble. In the future, Lizaveta Bogdanovna, don't be afraid of babblers: they're not dangerous. It's the silent ones, a bit touched, temperamental, with thick necks—they're the dangerous ones.

LIZAVETA

(After a pause) Tell me, is Natalya Petrovna really unwell?

SHPIGELSKY

As unwell as you and me.

LIZAVETA

She didn't eat anything at dinner.

SHPIGELSKY

Sickness isn't the only thing that spoils the appetite.

LIZAVETA

Did you dine at Bolshintsov's?

SHPIGELSKY

Yes . . . I went to see him. And came back only for your sake, by God.

LIZAVETA

Come now. Do you know what, Ignaty Ilyich? Natalya Petrovna's angry with you about something . . . What she said about you at the table wasn't exactly flattering.

SHPIGELSKY

Really? Evidently, ladies don't like it if we men have sharp eyes. Do everything their way, help them—and pretend all the while you don't understand them. That's how they are! Anyway, we'll see. Rakitin is probably in the dumps, too.

LIZAVETA

Yes, he's also not his old self today . . .

SHPIGELSKY

Hm. And Vera Alexandrovna? Belyaev?

LIZAVETA

Everybody, absolutely everybody, is out of sorts. I really don't know what's gotten into them all today.

SHPIGELSKY

Ignorance is bliss, Lizaveta Bogdanovna . . . Anyway, God be with them. Better talk about our own affairs. Shall we? You see, it's still raining . . .

LIZAVETA

(Lowering her eyes mincingly) What are you asking me, Ignaty Ilyich?

SHPIGELSKY

Lizaveta Bogdanovna, let me tell you something: why on earth do you keep simpering and lowering your eyes like that? You and I are not young people. These niceties, endearments, sighs—none of it suits us. Let's talk calmly, practically, as befits people our age. So, the question is this: we like each other . . . at least I assume you like me.

LIZAVETA

(Simpering slightly) Ignaty Ilyich, really . . .

SHPIGELSKY

Yes, yes, all right. As a woman, you even should . . . sort of . . . *(Gesturing with his hand)* . . . hedge a bit. So we like each other. And in other respects we also make a good pair. I must, of course, say of myself that I don't have a high pedigree; but then you're no aristocrat either. I'm not a rich man; otherwise I could just sort of . . . *(Smiles)* But I have a decent practice, not all my patients drop dead. You, from what you tell me, have fifteen thousand in cash. All that, you see, is not too bad. Besides, I imagine you're sick of being an eternal governess. And this fussing over the old woman, playing cards with her, and "yessing" her in everything, also can't be much fun. For my part, it's not that I'm bored with bachelor life, but I'm getting older, and besides the cooks rob me. So, you see, it all falls together very nicely. But here's the catch, Lizaveta Bogdanovna: you and I don't know each other at all. That is, to tell the truth, you don't know me . . . I do know you. I'm familiar with your character. I won't say there are no shortcomings to be found in you. Your maidenly life has soured you a little, but that's no matter. For a good husband, his wife is like soft wax. But I want you to know me, too, before the marriage; otherwise you might start blaming me afterwards . . . I don't want to mislead you.

LIZAVETA

(With dignity) But, Ignaty Ilyich, I believe I have also had a chance to become familiar with your character . . .

SHPIGELSKY

You? Oh, come now . . . That's not women's business. For instance, you think I'm a cheerful, jolly fellow—right?

LIZAVETA

To me you've always seemed a very agreeable man . . .

SHPIGELSKY

There you have it. You see how easy it is to be mistaken. Because I clown around with other people, tell them jokes, fawn on them, you've decided I'm really a cheerful man. If I didn't need these other people, I wouldn't even look at them . . . Whenever I can, without any risk, I make fun of them . . . But I'm not fooling myself. I know that certain people, who need me at every step, who are bored without me, think they have the right to despise me. And I pay them back in kind. Take Natalya Petrovna . . . You think I don't see through her? *(Imitating Natalya Petrovna)* "My dear doctor, I really do like you so much . . . you have such a wicked tongue . . ." heh, heh, coo away, my dove, coo away. Ohh, these ladies! They smile at you, and narrow their eyes at you, and there's disgust written all over their faces . . . We make them squeamish, but what can you do? I know why she said bad things about me today. Really, these ladies are amazing! Because they douse themselves with perfume each day and speak so carelessly, as if letting the words drop—here, pick that up!—they think they can get away with anything. But they can't! They're the same mortals as us sinners!

LIZAVETA

Ignaty Ilyich . . . You surprise me.

SHPIGELSKY

I knew I'd surprise you. So you see, I'm not that cheerful, maybe not even very nice . . . But with you I don't want to pass myself off as somebody I'm not. I may clown around with these people, but they know I'm no buffoon. Nobody's ever thrown a pie in my face. I could even say they're a little afraid of me. They know

I can bite. Once, some three years ago, a certain gentleman of the dumb farmer type was fool enough to smear horseradish in my hair at the table. What do you think? Right there and then, without getting angry, in the most courteous way, I challenged him to a duel. The dumb farmer nearly had a heart attack; the host made him apologize—the effect was extraordinary! I must admit, I knew beforehand he'd never fight. So you see, Lizaveta Bogdanovna, I'm as vain as they come; but this is how my life has turned out. I also have no great talents . . . As a student, I was so-so. I'm a bad doctor, there's no point hiding it from you; if you get sick, it won't be me who treats you. If I had talent and education, I'd have skipped off to the capital. But, of course, the locals don't need any better. As for my personal character, I must warn you, Lizaveta Bogdanovna, that at home I'm sullen, taciturn, demanding; I don't mind being well served and well gratified; I like my habits to be noted and my food to be tasty. On the other hand, I'm not jealous or stingy, and when I'm away, you can do whatever you like. You realize that there's no point talking about any sort of romantic love between us; still, I suppose it's possible to live under the same roof with me . . . As long as I'm gratified and there's no weeping in my presence, because I can't stand tears! And I don't nag. There's my confession. Well, ma'am, what do you say now?

LIZAVETA

What can I say, Ignaty Ilyich . . . If you've blackened yourself for some reason . . .

SHPIGELSKY

How have I blackened myself? Don't forget that another man in my place would quite calmly have said nothing about his shortcomings, seeing that you hadn't noticed anything, and after the wedding, tut-tut, it's too late. But I have too much pride for that.

Lizaveta Bogdanovna glances up at him.

Yes, too much pride . . . look at me all you want. I have no intention of pretending and lying before my future wife, not only for fifteen, but even for a hundred thousand. But I'll grovel before a stranger for a sack of flour. That's my character . . . With a stranger I'm all smiles, but I think to myself: what an imbecile you are, brother, to swallow such bait. But with you I say what I think. That is, allow me, I don't say all I think with you either, but at least I don't deceive you. I must seem like a great eccentric to you, but just wait, some day I'll tell you my life story: you'll be amazed that I'm still more or less in one piece. I don't suppose you ate off of gold dishes as a child either, but even so, my dove, you can't imagine what real, hardened poverty is . . . I'll tell you all about it some other time. Now you'd better think over what I've had the honor of laying out before you . . . Consider the little matter carefully, on your own, and tell me your decision. You are, as far as I've been able to see, a sensible woman. You . . . By the way, how old are you?

LIZAVETA

I'm . . . I'm . . . thirty.

SHPIGELSKY

(Calmly) That's not true: you're all of forty.

LIZAVETA

(Flaring up) Not forty at all. I'm thirty-six.

SHPIGELSKY

Still, that's not thirty. That's something you ought to give up, Lizaveta Bogdanovna . . . the more so as a married woman is not old at all at thirty-six. And you also shouldn't take snuff. *(Gets up)* The rain seems to have stopped.

LIZAVETA

(Also getting up) Yes, it has.

SHPIGELSKY

So, you'll give me an answer one of these days?

LIZAVETA

I'll tell you my decision tomorrow.

SHPIGELSKY

That I like! . . . That's really smart! There's my Lizaveta Bogdanovna! Well, give me your arm. Let's go back.

LIZAVETA

(Giving him her arm) Yes, let's.

SHPIGELSKY

By the way, I haven't kissed your hand . . . and it seems to be called
for . . . Well, why not this once!

He kisses her hand. Lizaveta Bogdanovna blushes.

There.

They go toward the door to the garden.

LIZAVETA

(Stopping) So you think Mikhail Alexandrych is not a dangerous
man?

SHPIGELSKY

So I think.

LIZAVETA

Do you know what, Ignaty Ilyich? It seems to me that for a while
now, Natalya Petrovna . . . it seems to me that Mr. Belyaev . . . She's
been paying attention to him . . . eh? And Verochka, too, don't you
think? That's why today . . .

SHPIGELSKY

(Interrupting her) I forgot to tell you one other thing, Lizaveta Bogdanovna. I'm a very inquisitive man, but I can't stand inquisitive

women. Let me explain: in my opinion, a wife should keep her eyes and ears open—that can even be very useful for her husband—but only with others . . . You understand: with others. However, if you absolutely must know what I think about Natalya Petrovna, Vera Alexandrovna, Mr. Belyaev and everybody else around here, listen then, I'll sing you a little song. I have a most vile voice, forgive me.

LIZAVETA

(Surprised) A little song!

SHPIGELSKY

Listen. First verse:

There once was a granny with a little gray goat,
There once was a granny with a little gray goat,
Hop one! hop two! little gray goat!
Hop one! hop two! little gray goat!

Second verse:

The little gray goat thought he'd go to the woods,
The little gray goat thought he'd go to the woods,
Hop one! hop two! go to the woods!
Hop one! hop two! go to the woods!

LIZAVETA

I really don't understand . . .

SHPIGELSKY

Listen, now. Third verse:

The gray wo-olves ate the wee little goat,
The gray wo-olves ate the wee little goat,
(Jumping up and down) Hop one! hop two! ate the wee goat!
Hop one! hop two! ate the wee goat!

And now let's go. By the way, I have something to talk over with Natalya Petrovna. I hope she won't bite. Unless I'm wrong, she still has need of me. Let's go.

They exit to the garden.

KATYA

(Warily coming from behind the column) They just wouldn't leave! What a nasty one that doctor is . . . talked and talked, and the things he said! And that singing! I'm afraid Alexei Nikolaich may have gone back to the house by now . . . They just had to come right here! *(Goes to the window)* And Lizaveta Bogdanovna? She'll be a doctor's wife . . . *(Laughs)* Think of it . . . I don't envy her . . . *(Looks out the window)* The grass has been washed so nicely . . . What a good smell . . . It's the bird cherry that smells like that . . . Ah, here he comes. *(Waiting a little)* Alexei Nikolaich! . . . Alexei Nikolaich! . . .

BELYAEV

(From off) Who's calling? Ah, it's you, Katya. *(Comes to the window)* What do you want?

KATYA

Come inside . . . I have something to tell you.

BELYAEV

Ah! All right. *(Leaves the window and a moment later comes in the door)* Here I am.

KATYA

Did you get caught in the rain?

BELYAEV

No . . . I sat in the greenhouse with Potap . . . he's your uncle, isn't he?

139

KATYA

Yes, sir, he is.

BELYAEV

How pretty you are today!

Katya smiles and lowers her eyes. He takes a peach from his pocket.

Would you like a peach?

KATYA

(Refusing) No, thank you very much . . . eat it yourself.

BELYAEV

Did I refuse when you offered me raspberries yesterday? Take it . . .
I picked it for you . . . I did.

KATYA

Thank you, then. *(Takes the peach)*

BELYAEV

That's better. So what did you want to tell me?

KATYA

The young miss . . . Vera Alexandrovna asked me . . . She wishes
to see you.

BELYAEV

Ah! I'll go to her at once.

KATYA

No, sir . . . She'll come here herself. She needs to have a talk with
you.

BELYAEV

(With some astonishment) She'll come here?

KATYA

Yes, sir. Here, you know . . . Nobody comes here. You won't be interrupted . . . *(Sighs)* She loves you very much, Alexei Nikolaich . . . She's so kind. I'll go and get her now, shall I? Will you wait?

BELYAEV

Of course, of course.

KATYA

One minute . . . *(Starts out, then stops)* Alexei Nikolaich, is it true what they say, that you're leaving us?

BELYAEV

Me? No . . . Who told you?

KATYA

So you're not leaving? Well, thank God! *(With embarrassment)* We'll be back in a minute.

Exits through the door to the house.

BELYAEV

(Remains motionless for a while) Amazing! Amazing things are happening to me! I never expected all this . . . Vera loves me . . . Natalya Petrovna knows . . . Vera has confessed everything to her . . . Amazing! Vera—such a dear, kind child; but then . . . what does this note mean? *(Takes a small scrap of paper from his pocket)* From Natalya Petrovna . . . in pencil. "Don't leave, don't decide anything until I have a talk with you." What does she want to talk with me about? *(Pause)* Where do I get these stupid ideas?! I find this all extremely embarrassing. If somebody had told me a month ago that I . . . I . . . I can't get over that talk with Natalya Petrovna. What makes my heart beat like this? And now Vera wants to see me . . . What will I say? At least I'll find out what it's all about . . . Maybe Natalya Petrovna is angry with me? . . . But why? *(Studies the note again)* It's strange, very strange.

The door opens quietly. He quickly hides the note. Vera and Katya appear on the threshold. He goes to them. Vera is very pale. She does not raise her eyes or move from the spot.

KATYA

Don't be afraid, miss. Go to him. I'll keep watch . . . Don't be afraid. *(To Belyaev)* Ah, Alexei Nikolaich!

She closes the windows, exits to the garden, and closes the door behind her.

BELYAEV

Vera Alexandrovna . . . you wanted to see me. Come here, sit down.

He takes her by the hand and leads her to the bench. Vera sits down.

There, now. *(Looking at her in astonishment)* You've been crying?

VERA

(Not raising her eyes) It's nothing . . . I've come to ask your forgiveness, Alexei Nikolaich.

BELYAEV

For what?

VERA

I've heard . . . you had an unpleasant talk with Natalya Petrovna . . . You're leaving . . . You've been dismissed.

BELYAEV

Who told you that?

VERA

Natalya Petrovna herself . . . I saw her after your talk. She told me you don't want to stay here any longer. But I think you've been dismissed.

BELYAEV

Tell me, do they know about it in the house?

VERA

No . . . Only Katya . . . I had to tell her . . . I wanted to talk with you, to ask your forgiveness. Now imagine how painful it must be for me . . . I'm the cause of it all, Alexei Nikolaich. I alone am to blame.

BELYAEV

You, Vera Alexandrovna?

VERA

I never expected . . . that Natalya Petrovna . . . But I can excuse her. You must excuse me, too . . . This morning I was a stupid child, but now . . . *(Stops herself)*

BELYAEV

Nothing's been decided yet, Vera Alexandrovna . . . Maybe I'll stay.

VERA

(Sadly) You say nothing's been decided, Alexei Nikolaich . . . No, everything's been decided, everything's over. See how you are with me now; and remember, just yesterday, in the garden . . . *(Pause)* Oh, I see Natalya Petrovna has told you everything.

BELYAEV

(With embarrassment) Vera Alexandrovna . . .

VERA

She's told you everything, I see it . . . She wanted to snare me, and I stupidly threw myself into her net . . . But she also gave herself away . . . I'm not such a child after all. *(Lowering her voice)* Oh, no!

BELYAEV

What are you trying to say?

VERA

(Glancing at him) Alexei Nikolaich, you want to leave us, is that correct?

BELYAEV

Yes.

VERA

Why?

Belyaev is silent.

You won't answer me?

BELYAEV

You weren't mistaken, Vera Alexandrovna . . . Natalya Petrovna has told me everything.

VERA

(In a weak voice) What, for instance.

BELYAEV

Vera Alexandrovna . . . It's really impossible for me . . . You understand.

VERA

Maybe she told you that I love you?

BELYAEV

(Hesitantly) Yes.

VERA

(Quickly) But it's not true . . .

BELYAEV

(With embarrassment) What?! . . .

VERA

(Covers her face with her hands and whispers hollowly through her fingers) At least I didn't tell her so, I don't remember . . . *(Raising her head)* She used me so cruelly! And you . . . that's why you want to leave?

BELYAEV

Vera Alexandrovna, judge for yourself . . .

VERA

(Glancing at him) He doesn't love me! *(Covers her face again)*

BELYAEV

(Sits down beside her and tries to take her hand) Vera Alexandrovna, give me your hand . . . Listen, I don't want any misunderstandings between us. I love you like a sister; I love you because it's impossible not to love you. Forgive me if I . . . Never in my life have I been in a situation like this . . . I wouldn't want to hurt you . . . I won't start pretending; I know that you like me, that you've fallen in love with me . . . But what can come of it? Judge for yourself. I'm only twenty, and I haven't got a penny to my name. Please don't be angry with me. I really don't know what to say to you.

VERA

(Taking her hands from her face and looking at him) My God, as if I'm asking for anything! But to be so cruel, so merciless . . . *(She stops herself)*

BELYAEV

I didn't want to upset you, Vera Alexandrovna.

VERA

I'm not blaming you, Alexei Nikolaich. You're not to blame for anything! I'm the one to blame . . . And I'm punished for it! I don't blame her either; I know she's a good woman, but she couldn't help herself . . . She was confused.

BELYAEV

(Perplexed) Confused?

VERA

(Turning to him) Natalya Petrovna loves you, Belyaev.

BELYAEV

What?!

VERA

She's in love with you.

BELYAEV

What are you saying?

VERA

I know what I'm saying. I've become old today . . . I'm no longer a child, believe me. She took it into her head to be jealous . . . of me! *(With a bitter smile)* How does that strike you?

BELYAEV

It can't be!

VERA

Can't be . . . Why, then, did she suddenly get the idea of marrying me off to this gentleman, what's his name—Bolshintsov? Why did she send the doctor to me, why did she try to persuade me herself? I know what I'm saying! If you could have seen, Belyaev, how her whole face changed when I told her . . . Oh, you can't imagine how cleverly, how cunningly she wheedled that confession out of me . . . Yes, she loves you; it's so clear . . .

BELYAEV

Vera Alexandrovna, you're mistaken, I assure you.

VERA

No, I'm not mistaken. Believe me, I'm not mistaken. If she doesn't love you, why did she torture me like that? What have I done to her? *(Bitterly)* Jealousy excuses everything. What's there to talk about! . . . And now, why is she dismissing you? She thinks that you . . . that you and I . . . Oh, she needn't worry! You can stay! *(Covers her face with her hands)*

BELYAEV

She hasn't dismissed me yet, Vera Alexandrovna . . . I told you nothing's decided yet . . .

VERA

(Suddenly raises her head and looks at him) Really?

BELYAEV

Yes . . . but why are you looking at me that way?

VERA

(As if to herself) Ah! I see . . . Yes, yes . . . she still hopes . . .

The door to the corridor opens quickly and Natalya Petrovna appears on the threshold. Seeing Vera and Belyaev, she stops.

BELYAEV

What are you saying?

VERA

Yes, now it's all clear to me . . . She's come to her senses, she's realized that I'm no threat to her. And, in fact, what am I? A stupid little girl, while she! . . .

BELYAEV

Vera Alexandrovna, how can you think . . .

VERA

And, finally, who knows? Maybe she's right . . . maybe you do love her . . .

BELYAEV

Me?

VERA

(Getting up) Yes, you. Why are you blushing?

BELYAEV

Me, Vera Alexandrovna?

VERA

Do you love her? Could you fall in love with her? You won't answer my question?

BELYAEV

But, for pity's sake, what kind of answer do you want? Vera Alexandrovna, you're so upset . . . Please calm down . . .

VERA

(Turning away from him) You treat me like a child . . . You don't even deign to answer me seriously . . . You just want to get rid of me . . . You think you can comfort me! *(She goes to leave, but suddenly stops, seeing Natalya Petrovna)* Natalya Petrovna . . .

Belyaev quickly turns to look.

NATALYA

(Taking several steps forward) Yes, it's me. *(She speaks with some effort)* I've come for you, Verochka.

VERA

(Slowly and coldly) What made you think of coming precisely here? Does it mean you've been looking for me?

NATALYA

Yes, I've been looking for you. You're imprudent, Verochka . . . I've told you more than once . . . And you, Alexei Nikolaich, have forgotten your promise . . . You have deceived me.

VERA

Enough of that, Natalya Petrovna! Stop it!

Natalya Petrovna looks at her in amazement.

Stop talking to me like a child . . . *(Lowering her voice)* I'm a woman now . . . As much of a woman as you are.

NATALYA

(Embarrassed) Vera . . .

VERA

(Almost in a whisper) He hasn't deceived you . . . He didn't ask for this meeting with me. He doesn't love me, you know that, so you needn't be jealous.

NATALYA

(With increasing amazement) Vera!

VERA

Believe me . . . stop pretending. This pretending no longer serves any purpose . . . I see through it now. Believe me. I'm not your ward, Natalya Petrovna, whom you look after *(Ironically)* like an older sister . . . *(Moves toward her)* I am your rival.

NATALYA

You forget yourself, Vera . . .

VERA

Maybe so . . . but who drove me to it? I don't know where I get the courage to speak to you like this . . . Maybe I'm speaking like this because I don't hope for anything anymore, because you so kindly walked all over me . . . And you succeeded . . . completely. But listen: I'm not going to be devious with you, as you were with me . . . know, then, that I've told him everything. *(Pointing at Belyaev)*

NATALYA

What could you have told him?

VERA

What? *(Ironically)* Oh, everything I've managed to notice. You hoped to wheedle everything out of me without giving yourself away. You were mistaken, Natalya Petrovna. You overestimated yourself . . .

NATALYA

Vera, Vera, come to your senses . . .

VERA

(In a whisper, and going still closer to her) Tell me I'm mistaken . . . Tell me you don't love him . . . Didn't he tell me that he didn't love me?

Natalya Petrovna is too embarrassed to say anything. Vera remains motionless for a while, then suddenly puts her hand to her forehead.

Natalya Petrovna, forgive me . . . I . . . I don't know . . . what's the matter with me, forgive me, don't be too hard on me . . . *(Dissolves in tears and quickly exits through the door to the corridor. Silence)*

BELYAEV

(Going to Natalya Petrovna) I assure you, Natalya Petrovna . . .

NATALYA

(Staring fixedly at the floor, holds her arm out in his direction) Stop, Alexei Nikolaich. It's true . . . Vera's right . . . It's time . . . I stopped being devious. I'm guilty before her, before you both . . . you have the right to despise me.

Belyaev makes an involuntary movement.

I've lowered myself in my own eyes. I have only one way left to win back your respect: frankness, complete frankness, whatever the consequences. Besides, I'm seeing you now for the last time, talking with you for the last time. I love you. *(She still does not look at him)*

BELYAEV

You, Natalya Petrovna! . . .

NATALYA

Yes, me. I love you. Vera was not deceived and did not deceive you. I fell in love with you the day you arrived, but I found it out only yesterday. I'm not going to justify my behavior . . . It was unworthy of me . . . but now at least you can understand, you can excuse me. Yes, I was jealous of Vera. Yes, in my mind I married her off to Bolshintsov to get her away from me and from you. Yes, I used the advantages of my age, my position, to wheedle her secret out of her, and—of course, I didn't expect it—I gave myself away. I love you, Belyaev, but know this: self-respect alone makes me confess it . . . the comedy I've been playing up to now revolts me. You can't stay here . . . However, after what I've just told you, you'll probably feel very awkward with me. You'll want to go away as soon as you can. I'm sure of it. That assurance makes me bold. I admit, I didn't want you to go away with a bad memory of me. Now you know everything . . . Maybe I interfered with you . . . maybe if all this hadn't happened, you'd have fallen in love with Verochka . . . I have only one excuse, Alexei Nikolaich . . . It was out of my control.

She falls silent. She says all this in a very even and calm voice, without looking at Belyaev. He is silent. She goes on with some agitation, still without looking at him.

You don't say anything? . . . Well, I understand. You have nothing to say to me. If a man who is not in love hears a declaration of love, it's very painful. I thank you for your silence. Believe me, when I told you . . . that I love you, I was not being devious . . . like before. I wasn't counting on anything. On the contrary, I wanted, finally, to tear off the mask, which, to be honest, didn't suit me at all . . . And, then, why go on playacting, when everything's known? Why pretend, if there's nobody left to deceive? It's all over between us now. I'm no longer keeping you. You may leave here without saying a word to me, without even a good-bye. I won't consider it impolite; on the contrary—I'll be grateful to you. There are cases in which delicacy is out of place . . . worse than rudeness. We obviously weren't fated to know each other. Good-bye. Yes, we weren't fated to know each other . . . but at least I hope that in your eyes I've now ceased to be that tyrannical, secretive and devious creature . . . Good-bye forever.

Belyaev is agitated, wants to say something, and cannot.

You're not going?

BELYAEV
(Bows, makes as if to leave, and, after some struggle with himself, comes back) No, I can't go . . .

Natalya Petrovna glances at him for the first time.

I can't go like this! . . . Listen, Natalya Petrovna, you just told me . . . you don't want me to go away with a bad memory of you, but I also don't want you to remember me as a man who . . . My God! I don't know how to say it . . . Forgive me, Natalya Petrovna . . . I don't know how to talk with ladies . . . Up to now I've known . . . a very different sort of women. You say we weren't fated to know each other, but, for pity's sake, could I, a simple, almost uneducated boy, even dream of becoming close to you? Think who you are and who I am! Think, could I dare to dream . . . Refined as you are . . . But what do I mean, refined . . . Look at me . . . this old jacket, and your scented dresses . . . Good God! Yes, I was afraid of you. I'm afraid of you even now . . . I looked at you, I'm not exaggerating, as a higher being, and yet . . . you, you tell me that you love me . . . you, Natalya Petrovna! Me! . . . I feel my heart beating as it's never beaten in all my life. It's beating not just because I'm amazed, it's not because I feel flattered . . . no! . . . it's something else now . . . But I . . . whatever you like, but I can't just go like this!

NATALYA
(After a pause, as if to herself) What have I done!

BELYAEV

Natalya Petrovna, for God's sake, believe me . . .

NATALYA

(In a changed voice) Alexei Nikolaich, if I didn't know you to be
an honorable man, a man incapable of lying, I might think God
knows what. I might regret having been so frank. But I trust you.
I don't want to hide my feelings from you: I'm grateful to you for
what you've just said to me. I now know why we didn't become
closer . . . It wasn't that you found me personally repellent . . . It
was only my position . . . *(Stops)* It's better this way, of course . . .
now it will be easier for me to give you up . . . Good-bye.

She makes as if to leave.

BELYAEV

(After a pause) Natalya Petrovna, I know I can't stay here . . . but
I can't tell you all that's going on inside me. You love me . . . it
frightens me even to say those words . . . it's all so new to me . . .
it's as if I'm seeing you and hearing you for the first time, but one
thing I do feel: I must leave . . . I feel that anything can happen . . .

NATALYA

(In a weak voice) Yes, Belyaev, you must leave . . . Now, after what
we've said, you must leave . . . And can it really be that, despite
everything I've done . . . Believe me, if I could even have remotely
suspected all you've just said to me—that confession would have
died in me . . . I only wanted to end all the misunderstandings,
I wanted to repent, to punish myself, I wanted to break the last
thread just like that. If I could have imagined . . . *(She covers her
face with her hands)*

BELYAEV

I believe you, Natalya Petrovna, I believe you. Take me: just fifteen
minutes ago . . . how could I have imagined . . . It was only today,
when we talked before lunch, that I felt for the first time something

extraordinary, indescribable, as if somebody's hand was squeezing my heart, and my chest was so hot . . . Before I did sort of avoid you, as if I even disliked you; but when you told me today that Vera Alexandrovna imagined . . . *(He stops)*

NATALYA

(With an involuntary smile of happiness) Enough, enough, Belyaev. We mustn't even think of it. We mustn't forget that we're speaking to each other for the last time . . . that you're leaving tomorrow . . .

BELYAEV

Yes! I'm leaving tomorrow! While I'm still able . . . This will all pass . . . I don't want to make too much of it . . . I'll leave . . . and then, as God wills! I'll take one memory with me, I'll always remember that you loved me . . . But why didn't I get to know you sooner? You're looking at me now . . . Can it be that I used to avoid your eyes? Can it be that I was ever shy with you? . . .

NATALYA

(Smiling) You just told me you were afraid of me.

BELYAEV

Did I? *(Pause)* Right . . . I'm surprised at myself . . . Me, me talking to you like this? I don't recognize myself.

NATALYA

And you're not deceiving yourself?

BELYAEV

About what?

NATALYA

About you . . . me . . . *(Gives a start)* Oh, God! What am I doing . . . Listen, Belyaev . . . Help me . . . Has any woman ever been in a situation like this? I'm just not strong enough . . . Maybe it's for the best to break it all off at once, but at least we've come to know each other . . . Give me your hand—and good-bye forever.

BELYAEV

(Takes her hand) Natalya Petrovna . . . What can I say to you? . . . There's so much in my heart . . . God grant you . . . *(Stops and presses her hand to his lips)* Good-bye. *(Makes as if to leave through the garden door)*

NATALYA

(Following him with her eyes) Belyaev . . .

BELYAEV

(Turning) Natalya Petrovna . . .

NATALYA

(After a pause, in a weak voice) Stay . . .

BELYAEV

What?! . . .

NATALYA

Stay, and let God be our judge! *(She buries her face in her hands)*

BELYAEV

(Quickly goes to her and holds out his arms to her) Natalya Petrovna . . .

Just then the door to the garden opens and Rakitin appears on the threshold. He looks at the two of them for a while and suddenly goes up to them.

RAKITIN

(Loudly) They're looking for you everywhere, Natalya Petrovna . . .

Natalya Petrovna and Belyaev turn to him.

NATALYA

(Taking her hands from her face, and as if coming to her senses) Ah, it's you . . . Who is looking for me?

Belyaev, embarrassed, bows to Natalya Petrovna and makes as if to leave.

Wait a minute, Alexei Nikolaich . . . don't forget, you know . . .

He bows a second time and exits to the garden.

RAKITIN

Arkady's looking for you . . . I must say, I didn't expect to find you here . . . but, I was passing by and . . .

NATALYA

(Smiling) Heard our voices . . . I met Alexei Nikolaich here . . . and had a little talk with him . . . Today seems to be the day for such talks. But we can go back now . . . *(Makes as if to exit through the door to the corridor)*

RAKITIN

(In some agitation) Can I know . . . what's been decided? . . .

NATALYA

(Pretending to be surprised) Decided? . . . I don't understand you.

RAKITIN

(After a long pause, sadly) In that case, I understand everything.

NATALYA

Well, there you go . . . Again these mysterious hints! Yes, I had a talk with him, and now everything's back in order again . . . It was all nothing, we made too much of it . . . Everything you and I talked about was just childish. It should be forgotten now.

RAKITIN

I'm not asking for details, Natalya Petrovna.

NATALYA

(With forced casualness) What was it I wanted to tell you . . . I don't remember. Never mind. Let's go. It's all over . . . all done with.

RAKITIN

(Giving her an intent look) Yes, it's all over. You must be quite annoyed with yourself now . . . for being so frank today . . . *(He turns away)*

NATALYA

Rakitin . . .

He glances at her again. She obviously does not know what to say.

Have you spoken with Arkady yet?

RAKITIN

No, ma'am. I haven't prepared anything yet . . . You understand, I have to make something up . . .

NATALYA

I can't stand it! What do they want from me! They follow my every footstep. Rakitin, really, I'm ashamed of myself . . .

RAKITIN

Oh, Natalya Petrovna, please don't worry . . . What for? That's the way it is. But it's so obvious that Mr. Belyaev is still a novice! Why did he get so embarrassed, run away? . . . However, in time . . . *(In a low voice and quickly)* The two of you will learn to pretend . . . *(Aloud)* Let's go.

Natalya Petrovna makes as if to go up to him and stops. Just then Islaev's voice comes from outside the door to the garden: "He went in here, you say?" and after that Islaev and Shpigelsky enter.

ISLAEV

Right . . . here he is. Well, well, well! And Natalya Petrovna's here, too! *(Going to her)* What's this, a continuation of today's talk? It's obviously an important subject.

RAKITIN

I ran into Natalya Petrovna here . . .

ISLAEV

Ran into her? *(Looks around)* A busy place, is it?

NATALYA

Well, you're here . . .

ISLAEV

I'm here because . . . *(Stops)*

NATALYA

You were looking for me?

ISLAEV

(After a pause) Yes, I was looking for you. Wouldn't you like to go back to the house? Tea's ready. It'll be dark soon.

NATALYA

(Takes his arm) Let's go.

ISLAEV

(Looking around) This could be turned into two good rooms for the gardeners—or more servants' quarters—what do you think, Shpigelsky?

SHPIGELSKY

Certainly.

ISLAEV

Let's go through the garden, Natasha.

They go to the garden door. During this scene he has not once glanced at Rakitin. On the threshold, he half turns.

What are you waiting for, gentlemen? Let's go and have tea.

Exits with Natalya Petrovna.

SHPIGELSKY

(To Rakitin) Well, Mikhail Alexandrych, let's go . . . Give me your arm . . . Evidently you and I are fated to be in the rearguard . . .

RAKITIN

(With vexation) May I tell you something, mister doctor? I'm awfully sick of you . . .

SHPIGELSKY

(With feigned good-naturedness) If you only knew, Mikhail Alexandrych, how sick I am of myself!

Rakitin smiles involuntarily.

Let's go, let's go . . .

They both exit through the garden door.
   Curtain.

ACT FIVE

Morning of the next day. The same decor as in the first and third acts. Islaev sits at the table looking through some papers. He suddenly gets up.

ISLAEV

No! I really can't work today. It's like a nail's been driven into my head. *(Paces the room)* I must say I didn't expect this; I didn't expect I'd be as upset . . . as I am now. What am I supposed to do? . . . that's the problem. *(Ponders, then suddenly shouts)* Matvei!

MATVEI

(Enters) What is it, sir?

ISLAEV

Send for the foreman . . . And tell the diggers at the dam to wait for me . . . Off you go.

MATVEI

Yes, sir. *(Exits)*

ISLAEV

(Going to the table again and leafing through the papers) Yes . . .
the problem!

ANNA

(Entering and going to Islaev) Arkasha!

ISLAEV

Ah, it's you, mama. How are you today?

ANNA

(Sitting down on the sofa) I'm well, thank God. *(Sighs)* I'm well.
(Sighs louder) Thank God. *(Seeing that Islaev is not listening to
her, she sighs very loudly, with a slight moan)*

ISLAEV

You're sighing . . . What's the matter?

ANNA

(Sighs again, but not so loudly now) Ah, Arkasha, as if you don't
know why I'm sighing!

ISLAEV

What do you mean?

ANNA

(After a pause) I'm your mother, Arkasha. Of course, you're a
grown-up, reasonable man, but still—I'm your mother. It's a great
word: mother!

ISLAEV

Kindly explain yourself.

ANNA

You know what I'm hinting at, my dear. Your wife, Natasha . . . of
course, she's an excellent woman—and her behavior up to now has
been quite exemplary . . . but she's still so young, Arkasha! And
youth . . .

ISLAEV

I see what you want to say . . . You think her relationship with Rakitin . . .

ANNA

God forbid! I never thought . . .

ISLAEV

You didn't let me finish . . . You think her relationship with Rakitin is not quite . . . clear. These secret conversations, these tears—you find it all a bit strange.

ANNA

Arkasha, has he finally told you what those conversations between them were about? . . . He's said nothing to me.

ISLAEV

I haven't asked him any questions, mama, and he's obviously in no hurry to satisfy my curiosity.

ANNA

What are you going to do now?

ISLAEV

Me, mama? Why, nothing.

ANNA

What do you mean, nothing?

ISLAEV

Just that: nothing.

ANNA

(Getting up) I must say that surprises me. Of course, you're the master in your own house, and you know better than I do what's good and what's bad. But think of the consequences . . .

ISLAEV

Mama, really, you're getting upset over nothing.

ANNA

My dear boy, I am your mother . . . but you know best. *(Pause)*
I confess, I came intending to offer my assistance . . .

ISLAEV

(Hastily) No, mama, I beg you not to trouble yourself about it . . .
Do me a favor!

ANNA

As you wish, Arkasha, as you wish. I won't say another word. I've
warned you, I've done my duty—and now—I hold my tongue.

A brief silence.

ISLAEV

You're not going anywhere today?

ANNA

Only I must warn you: you're too trusting, my dear; you judge
everybody by yourself! Believe me: real friends are all too rare in
our time!

ISLAEV

(Impatiently) Mama . . .

ANNA

Well—no more, no more! I'm just an old woman. I suppose I'm
getting senile. I was brought up on different principles. I tried to
instill them into you . . . All right, work, I won't bother you . . . I'll
leave. *(Goes to the door and stops)* So, then? . . . Well, you know
best, you know best. *(Exits)*

ISLAEV

(Following her with his eyes) What makes people who really love
you stick all their fingers into your wound one after the other? And

they're convinced it makes you feel better—that's the funny part! But I'm not blaming mother: she really means well—and how can she help giving advice? But that's not the point . . . *(Sitting down)* What am I supposed to do? *(He ponders, then gets up)* Eh, the simpler the better! Diplomatic subtleties don't suit me . . . I'll be the first to get tangled up in them.

He rings the bell. Matvei enters.

Do you know if Mikhail Alexandrych is around?

MATVEI

He is, sir. I just saw him in the billiard room.

ISLAEV

Ah! Well, then ask him to come here.

MATVEI

Yes, sir. *(Exits)*

ISLAEV

(Pacing back and forth) What a mess! I'm not used to this . . . Let's hope it won't happen often . . . I have a strong constitution—but I wouldn't survive that. *(Puts his hand to his chest)* Pah! . . .

Rakitin enters from the ballroom, embarrassed.

RAKITIN

You sent for me?

ISLAEV

Yes . . . *(Pause)* Michel, I believe you owe me something.

RAKITIN

Me?

ISLAEV

Who else? Have you forgotten your promise? About . . . Natasha's crying . . . and all that . . . When mama and I found you, remember—you told me there was a secret between you that you wanted to explain?

RAKITIN

Did I say "a secret"?

ISLAEV

You did.

RAKITIN

What sort of secret could there be? We were talking.

ISLAEV

About what? And why was she crying?

RAKITIN

You know, Arkady . . . there are moments in a woman's life . . . even the happiest woman . . .

ISLAEV

Wait, Rakitin, this isn't right. I can't bear to see you like this . . . Your embarrassment is more painful for me than for you. *(Takes him by the arm)* We're old friends—we've known each other since childhood: I don't know how to be devious—and you've always been frank with me, too. Let me ask you a question . . . I promise you on my honor, I won't doubt the sincerity of your answer. Do you love my wife?

Rakitin glances at Islaev.

You know what I mean: do you love her the way . . . Well, in short, do you love my wife in a way that would be . . . hard to admit to a husband?

RAKITIN

(After a pause, in a hollow voice) Yes, I love your wife . . . in that way.

ISLAEV

(Also after a pause) Thank you for your frankness, Michel. You're an honorable man. Well, so, what do we do now? Sit down, let's talk it over.

Rakitin sits down. Islaev paces the room.

I know Natasha; I know her worth . . . But I also know my own worth. I'm not as worthy as you, Michel . . . don't interrupt me, please—I am not as worthy as you. You're more intelligent, better, and, finally, nicer than I am. I'm a simple man. Natasha loves me—I think—but she has eyes . . . well, in short, how could she not like you? And I'll tell you another thing: I noticed your penchant for each other long ago . . . But I've always trusted you both—and so far nothing has come to light . . . Eh! I'm no good at talking! *(Pause)* But after that scene yesterday, after your second meeting in the evening—what am I to do? If only I'd been alone when I found you—but there were witnesses: mama, that rascal Shpigelsky . . . Well, what do you say, Michel—eh?

RAKITIN

You're perfectly right, Arkady.

ISLAEV

That's not the point . . . but what am I to do? I'll tell you, Michel, that although I'm a simple man, I know enough to understand that it's no good ruining other people's lives—and there are times when it's sinful to insist on your own rights. I didn't get that out of books, my friend . . . it's my conscience speaking. Set her free . . . well, so, set her free! Only this has to be thought through. It's much too important.

RAKITIN

(Getting up) I've already thought it through.

167

ISLAEV

And?

RAKITIN

I must leave . . . I'm leaving.

ISLAEV

(After a pause) You think so? . . . Just clear off?

RAKITIN

Yes.

ISLAEV

(Starts pacing back and forth again) That's . . . that's saying something! Maybe you're right. It'll be hard for us without you . . . God knows, it may not lead to anything . . . but you know better. I suppose that's the right idea . . . You're a danger to me, my friend . . . *(With a sad smile)* Yes . . . you're a danger to me. What I just said . . . about setting her free . . . I probably wouldn't survive it! Without Natasha, I . . . *(Waves his hand)* And here's another thing: for a while now, especially during these last few days, I've seen a big change in her. Some sort of deep, constant restlessness. It frightens me. Isn't it true? I'm not mistaken?

RAKITIN

(Bitterly) Oh, no, you're not mistaken!

ISLAEV

Well, there, you see! So you're leaving?

RAKITIN

Yes.

ISLAEV

Hm. And it all came so suddenly! Did you have to get so embarrassed when mother and I caught you?

MATVEI

(Enters) The foreman is here, sir.

ISLAEV

He can wait!

Matvei exits.

Anyway, Michel, you're not going for long, are you? This is all nothing!

RAKITIN

I don't really know . . . I think . . . it's for long.

ISLAEV

You don't take me for some sort of Othello? Really, I don't think there's been such a talk between two friends since the world began! I can't just part with you for good . . .

RAKITIN

(Pressing his hand) You'll let me know when I can come back.

ISLAEV

There's nobody here to take your place! Not Bolshintsov, certainly!

RAKITIN

There are others . . .

ISLAEV

Who? Krinitsyn? That peacock? Belyaev is a nice boy, of course, but he's as far from you as the earth from the sky!

RAKITIN

(Sarcastically) You think so? You don't know him, Arkady . . . You should pay more attention to him . . . That's my advice . . . Do you hear? He's a very . . . a very remarkable man!

ISLAEV

Well, so that's why you and Natasha wanted to busy yourselves with his education! *(Glancing out the door)* Huh, here he is! Coming this way . . . *(Hurriedly)* So, my friend, it's decided—you're leaving . . . for a little while . . . one of these days . . . There's no hurry—we have to prepare Natasha . . . I'll calm mama down . . . Bless you! You've taken a weight off my heart . . . Embrace me, my dear fellow! *(Hurriedly embraces him and turns to the entering Belyaev)* Ah . . . it's you! How are you doing?

BELYAEV

Very well, Arkady Sergeich.

ISLAEV

And where is Kolya?

BELYAEV

He's with Mr. Schaaf.

ISLAEV

Ah . . . excellent! *(Takes his hat)* Well, good-bye, then, gentlemen. I haven't been anywhere today—not to the dam, not to the building site . . . I haven't even looked over the papers. *(He grabs them and puts them under his arm)* Good-bye!—Matvei! Matvei! Come along!

He exits. Rakitin, pensive, remains where he is.

BELYAEV

(Going to Rakitin) How are you feeling today, Mikhail Alexandrych?

RAKITIN

Same as ever, thanks. And you?

BELYAEV

I'm well.

RAKITIN

That's obvious!

BELYAEV

How do you mean?

RAKITIN

Just . . . by the look of you . . . You've put on a new jacket today . . .
And . . . what's this I see! A flower in your buttonhole?

Belyaev blushes and pulls it out.

But why . . . why on earth . . . It's very sweet . . . *(Pause)* By the way,
Alexei Nikolaich, in case you need anything . . . I'm going to town
tomorrow.

BELYAEV

Tomorrow?

RAKITIN

Yes . . . and from there maybe to Moscow.

BELYAEV

(With surprise) To Moscow? I thought you told me just yesterday
that you were going to stay for about a month . . .

RAKITIN

Yes . . . but my affairs . . . something's come up . . .

BELYAEV

Will you be gone long?

RAKITIN

I don't know . . . maybe.

BELYAEV

May I ask if Natalya Petrovna knows of your intention?

171

RAKITIN

No, she doesn't. Why do you ask me especially about her?

BELYAEV

Me? *(Slightly embarrassed)* No reason.

RAKITIN

(After pausing and looking around) Alexei Nikolaich, it seems there's nobody in the room but us. Isn't it strange for us to be playing this comedy in front of each other, eh? What do you think?

BELYAEV

I don't understand you, Mikhail Alexandrych.

RAKITIN

Really? So you don't understand why I'm leaving?

BELYAEV

No.

RAKITIN

That's odd . . . But I'm prepared to believe you. Maybe you really don't know . . . Shall I tell you why I'm leaving?

BELYAEV

Please do.

RAKITIN

You see, Alexei Nikolaich—by the way, I'm trusting in your discretion—you just found me with Arkady Sergeich . . . He and I were having a rather important talk. It's precisely because of that talk that I've decided to leave. And do you know why? I'm telling you all this because I consider you an honorable man . . . He imagined that I . . . well, yes, that I'm in love with Natalya Petrovna. How does that strike you, eh? A strange idea, isn't it? But I'm grateful to him that he didn't start being devious, keeping an eye on us, or whatever, but simply came right out and asked me. Now tell me, what would you do in my place? Of course, there are no grounds

for his suspicions, but still they trouble him . . . A decent man
should be able to sacrifice . . . his pleasure for the sake of a friend's
peace of mind. That's why I'm leaving . . . I'm sure you approve of
my decision, don't you? Wouldn't you do the same in my place?
Wouldn't you leave?

BELYAEV

(After a pause) Maybe so.

RAKITIN

I'm very pleased to hear that . . . Of course, I don't deny that there's
a ridiculous side to my leaving, as if I could really be a threat. But
you see, Alexei Nikolaich, a woman's honor is such an important
thing . . . And besides—not that I'm saying this about Natalya
Petrovna—but I've known pure women with innocent hearts, real
infants, for all their intelligence, who, precisely because of their
purity and innocence, have been more likely than anyone else to
surrender to a sudden passion . . . And so, who knows? Prudence
never hurts on such occasions, especially if . . . By the way, Alexei
Nikolaich, maybe you still think that there's no greater good on
earth than love?

BELYAEV

(Coldly) I haven't experienced that yet, but I think that being loved
by a woman you love is a great happiness.

RAKITIN

May you entertain such pleasant convictions for a long time! In
my opinion, Alexei Nikolaich, any love, happy or unhappy, is a
real calamity if you surrender to it completely . . . Just wait! Maybe
one day you'll learn how those sweet little hands can torture,
with what tender care they can tear your heart to shreds . . . Just
wait! You'll learn how much burning hatred is hidden behind the
most ardent love! You'll remember me, when you yearn for peace,
the most meaningless, the most banal peace, the way a sick man
yearns for health, when you envy any man who is light-hearted and

free . . . Just wait! You'll learn what it means to be tied to a skirt, what it means to be enslaved, infected—and how shameful and tedious that slavery is! . . . You'll learn, finally, that you've paid such a high price for mere trifles . . . But why am I telling you all this, you're not going to believe me now. The thing is that I'm very glad you approve . . . yes, yes . . . in such cases it's best to be cautious.

BELYAEV

(Who has not taken his eyes off Rakitin all the while) Thank you for the lesson, Mikhail Alexandrych, though I didn't need it.

RAKITIN

(Takes him by the arm) Please excuse me, I never meant . . . who am I to give anybody lessons? . . . I just started talking away . . .

BELYAEV

(With light irony) For no reason?

RAKITIN

(Slightly embarrassed) Precisely for no special reason. I only wanted . . . Up to now, Alexei Nikolaich, you've had no chance to study women. Women are a very peculiar species.

BELYAEV

Who are you talking about?

RAKITIN

Oh . . . nobody in particular.

BELYAEV

About all of them in general, is that it?

RAKITIN

(Forcing a smile) Yes, maybe. I really don't know what made me fall into this teacherly tone, but let me give you some good advice

174

before I go. *(Stops and waves his hand)* Eh! but what kind of adviser am I! Please excuse my babbling . . .

BELYAEV

On the contrary, on the contrary . . .

RAKITIN

So you don't need anything from town?

BELYAEV

Nothing, thank you. But I'm sorry you're leaving.

RAKITIN

I humbly thank you . . . I assure you that I, too, am . . .

Natalya Petrovna and Vera enter from the study. Vera is very sad and pale.

. . . very glad to have made your acquaintance. *(Shakes his hand again)*

NATALYA

(Looks at the two of them for some time, then goes up to them) Good morning, gentlemen.

RAKITIN

(Turning quickly) Good morning, Natalya Petrovna . . . Good morning, Vera Alexandrovna . . .

Belyaev silently bows to Natalya Petrovna and Vera. He is embarrassed.

NATALYA

(To Rakitin) What are you up to?

RAKITIN

Nothing really . . .

NATALYA

Vera and I have already taken a stroll in the garden . . . It's so nice out today . . . The lindens smell so sweet. We strolled about under the lindens . . . It's a pleasure to be in the shade and listen to the buzzing of the bees overhead . . . *(Timidly to Belyaev)* We hoped to meet you there.

Belyaev says nothing.

RAKITIN

(To Natalya Petrovna) Ah! So today you, too, are paying attention to the beauties of nature . . . *(Pause)* Alexei Nikolaich couldn't go to the garden . . . He's put on a new jacket today . . .

BELYAEV

(Flushing slightly) Of course, it's the only one I have, and I might tear it in the garden . . . Is that what you mean?

RAKITIN

(Turning red) Oh, no . . . not that at all . . .

Vera goes silently to the sofa at the right, sits down, and begins her handwork. Natalya Petrovna gives Belyaev a forced smile. A short, rather oppressive silence ensues. Rakitin goes on with sarcastic nonchalance.

Ah, yes, I forgot to tell you, Natalya Petrovna—I'm leaving today . . .

NATALYA

(With a certain agitation) Leaving? For where?

RAKITIN

For town . . . On business.

NATALYA

Not for long, I hope?

RAKITIN

Depends on the business.

NATALYA

See that you come back soon. *(To Belyaev, without looking at him)* Alexei Nikolaich, those drawings Kolya showed me, are they yours?

BELYAEV

Yes, ma'am . . . I . . . just doodles . . .

NATALYA

On the contrary, they're very nice. You have talent.

RAKITIN

I see you discover new virtues in Mr. Belyaev every day.

NATALYA

(Coldly) Maybe . . . So much the better for him. *(To Belyaev)* You probably have other drawings. You must show them to me.

Belyaev bows.

RAKITIN

(Who stands there all the while as if on pins and needles) Anyway, I think it's time I packed . . . Good-bye. *(Goes to the ballroom door)*

NATALYA

(After him) We'll still see you before you leave . . .

RAKITIN

Of course.

BELYAEV

(After some hesitation) Wait, Mikhail Alexandrych, I'll come with you. I have something to say to you . . .

RAKITIN

Ah!

177

Both exit to the ballroom. Natalya Petrovna remains standing; after a while, she goes and sits down.

NATALYA

(After a pause) Vera!

VERA

(Not raising her head) What do you want?

NATALYA

Vera, for God's sake, don't be like that with me . . . for God's sake, Vera . . . Verochka . . .

Vera says nothing. Natalya Petrovna gets up, crosses to her, and quietly kneels before her. Vera wants to make her stand up, turns away, and covers her face. Natalya Petrovna speaks while kneeling.

Vera, forgive me. Don't cry, Vera. I wronged you, I'm guilty. Can't you forgive me?

VERA

(Through her tears) Stand up, stand up . . .

NATALYA

I won't stand up until you forgive me, Vera. It's hard for you . . . but think, is it any easier for me? . . . Think, Vera . . . You know everything . . . The only difference between us is that you haven't wronged me, while I . . .

VERA

(Bitterly) The only difference! No, Natalya Petrovna, there's another difference between us . . . You're so gentle, so kind, so tender today . . .

NATALYA

(Interrupting her) Because I feel guilty . . .

VERA

Really? Only because of that . . .

NATALYA

(Gets up and sits next to her) What other reason could there be?

VERA

Don't torment me anymore, Natalya Petrovna, don't ask me any questions . . .

NATALYA

(Sighing) Vera, I see you can't forgive me.

VERA

You're so kind and gentle today, because you feel you're loved.

NATALYA

(Embarrassed) Vera!

VERA

(Turning to her) Isn't it true?

NATALYA

(Sadly) Believe me, I'm as unhappy as you are.

VERA

He loves you!

NATALYA

What's the point in tormenting each other, Vera? It's time we came to our senses. Remember what situation I'm in, what situation we're both in. Remember that our secret—because of me, of course—is already known to two people here . . . *(Stops)* Vera, instead of torturing each other with suspicions and reproaches, wouldn't it be better for us both to think how to get out of this painful situation . . . how to save ourselves? Or do you think I can bear all this worry, this anxiety? Have you forgotten who I am? You're not listening.

VERA

(Pensively looking at the floor) He loves you . . .

NATALYA

He's leaving, Vera.

VERA

(Turning to her) Oh, let me be . . .

Natalya Petrovna looks at her undecidedly. Just then Islaev's voice is heard from the study: "Natasha, Natasha, where are you?"

NATALYA

(Quickly gets up and goes to the door of the study) I'm here . . . What is it?

ISLAEV

(From off) Come here, I must tell you something . . .

NATALYA

Just a moment.

She goes back to Vera and holds out her hand to her. Vera does not move. Natalya Petrovna sighs and exits to the study.

VERA

(Alone, after a pause) He loves her! . . . And I have to go on living in her house . . . It's too much . . .

She covers her face with her hands and remains motionless. Shpigelsky's head appears through the ballroom door. He looks around warily and tiptoes toward Vera, who doesn't notice him.

SHPIGELSKY

(Stands before her with his arms crossed and a sarcastic smile on his face) Vera Alexandrovna! . . . Ahem, Vera Alexandrovna . . .

VERA

(Raising her head) Who's that? Ah, it's you, doctor . . .

SHPIGELSKY

What's wrong, miss? Are you unwell, or something?

VERA

No, it's nothing.

SHPIGELSKY

Let me feel your pulse. *(Feels her pulse)* Hm, why so quick? Ah, you, miss, my dear miss . . . You won't listen to me . . . And yet I only wish the best for you.

VERA

(Looking at him resolutely) Ignaty Ilyich . . .

SHPIGELSKY

(Promptly) I'm listening, Vera Alexandrovna . . . Good God, what a look . . . I'm listening.

VERA

This gentleman . . . your acquaintance, Bolshintsov, is he really a good man?

SHPIGELSKY

My friend Bolshintsov? A most excellent, a most honorable man . . . a model and example of virtue.

VERA

He's not wicked?

SHPIGELSKY

Good God, he's as kind as could be. He's not a man, he's a lump of dough. Good God, just take him and shape him. There's no kinder man in the world. A dove, not a man.

VERA

You vouch for him?

SHPIGELSKY

(Putting one hand on his heart and raising the other) As for my own self!

VERA

In that case, you may tell him . . . that I'm ready to marry him.

SHPIGELSKY

(With joyful amazement) Oh, my!

VERA

But as soon as possible—do you hear? As soon as possible . . .

SHPIGELSKY

Tomorrow, if you like . . . Well, now! That's my Vera Alexandrovna! Good for you, miss! I'll gallop to him at once. He'll be overjoyed . . . What an unexpected development! He simply adores you, Vera Alexandrovna . . .

VERA

(Impatiently) I'm not asking you that, Ignaty Ilyich.

SHPIGELSKY

Whatever you say, Vera Alexandrovna, whatever you say. Only you're going to be happy with him, you're going to thank me, you'll see . . .

Vera again makes an impatient gesture.

All right, no more, no more . . . So I can tell him . . .

VERA

Yes, yes.

SHPIGELSKY

Very good, miss. So I'll go right now. Good-bye. *(Listens)* Besides, somebody's coming. *(He goes toward the study, and on the threshold makes a grimace of private amazement)* Good-bye. *(Exits)*

VERA

(Looking after him) Anything's better than staying here . . . *(Gets up)* Yes, I've made up my mind. I won't stay in this house . . . not for anything. I can't bear her meek eyes, her smile, I can't stand how at ease she is, how she basks in her happiness. Because she *is* happy, however sad and melancholy she pretends to be . . . Her caresses are insufferable . . .

Belyaev appears from the door to the ballroom. He looks around and goes to Vera.

BELYAEV

(In a low voice) Vera Alexandrovna, are you alone?

VERA

(Looks at him, gives a start; after a brief pause) Yes.

BELYAEV

I'm glad . . . Otherwise I wouldn't come in. Vera Alexandrovna, I've come to say good-bye to you.

VERA

To say good-bye?

BELYAEV

Yes, I'm leaving.

VERA

Leaving? You're leaving, too?

IVAN TURGENEV

BELYAEV

Yes ... me, too. *(With strong inner agitation)* You see, Vera Alexandrovna, I can't stay. I've already caused a lot of trouble just by
being here. For one thing, I've disturbed the peace here for you
and Natalya Petrovna without knowing how. I've also broken up
old friendships. Thanks to me, Mr. Rakitin is leaving, and you have
quarreled with your guardian ... It's time to put a stop to it all.
After I'm gone, I hope everything will settle down and fall back
into place ... Turning the heads of rich ladies and young girls is
not for me ... You'll forget about me, and in time you may even
be surprised at how it all could have happened ... It surprises me
even now ... I'll tell you the truth, Vera Alexandrovna: it's frightening, it's even eerie to think of staying ... Anything can happen ...
You know, I'm not used to all this. It's awkward for me ... it feels
like everybody's looking at me ... And, finally, it would be impossible for me ... now ... with the two of you ...

VERA

Oh, don't worry about me! I won't be here for long.

BELYAEV

How's so?

VERA

That's my secret. But I won't get in your way, believe me.

BELYAEV

So, you see, how can I not leave? Judge for yourself. It's like I've
brought a plague on this house: everybody's fleeing the place ...
Isn't it better for me alone to disappear while there's still time? I've
just had a big talk with Mr. Rakitin ... You can't imagine how bitter he sounds ... He teased me about my new jacket, and it served
me right ... Yes, I've got to leave. Believe me, Vera Alexandrovna,
I can't wait for the moment when I go galloping in a cart down
the high road ... I'm suffocating here, I need air. I can't tell you
how bad I feel and at the same time how relieved, like a man set-

ting out on a long journey across the sea: he's heartsick at leaving his friends, he's scared, and yet the noise of the sea is so cheerful, the wind blowing in his face is so fresh, that the blood rises in his veins, no matter how heavy his heart is . . . Yes, I'm set on leaving. I'll go back to Moscow, to my friends, I'll work . . .

VERA

So you love her, Alexei Nikolaich; you love her, and yet you're leaving.

BELYAEV

Stop, Vera Alexandrovna, what's the point? Don't you see it's all over? All. It flashed and went out like a spark. Let's part friends. It's time. I've come to my senses. Be well, be happy, some day we'll see each other . . . I'll never forget you, Vera Alexandrovna . . . I've grown very fond of you, believe me . . . *(He presses her hand and adds hastily)* Give Natalya Petrovna this note from me . . .

VERA

(Glancing at him in embarrassment) Note?

BELYAEV

Yes . . . I can't say good-bye to her.

VERA

You mean you're leaving right now?

BELYAEV

Right now . . . I haven't told anybody . . . except Mikhail Alexandrych. He approves. I'll go from here to Petrovskoe on foot. In Petrovskoe I'll wait for Mikhail Alexandrych, and we'll drive to town together. I'll write from town. My belongings will be sent on to me. You see, everything's already arranged . . . Anyway, you can read the note. It's just a couple of words.

VERA

(Taking the note) So you're really leaving? . . .

185

BELYAEV

Yes, yes . . . Give her this note and tell her . . . no, don't tell her anything. What for? *(Listening)* Somebody's coming. Good-bye . . .

*He rushes to the door, stops on the threshold for a moment, and runs
out. Vera stays, the note in her hand. Natalya Petrovna enters from
the ballroom.*

NATALYA

(Going to Vera) Verochka . . . *(Looks at her and stops)* What's the
matter with you?

Vera silently hands her the note.

A note? . . . Who from?

VERA

(Hollowly) Read it.

NATALYA

You frighten me.

*She reads the note to herself and suddenly presses both hands to her
face and falls into the armchair. A long pause.*

VERA

(Going to her) Natalya Petrovna . . .

NATALYA

(Not taking her hands from her face) He's gone! . . . He didn't even
want to say good-bye to me . . . At least he said good-bye to you!

VERA

(Sadly) He didn't love me . . .

NATALYA

(Taking her hands from her face and getting up) But he has no right
to leave like this . . . I want . . . He can't just . . . Who told him he

could break it off so stupidly . . . What contempt! . . . I . . . how does he know I'd never decide . . . *(Lowers herself into the armchair)* My God, my God . . .

VERA

Natalya Petrovna, you just said to me yourself that he had to leave . . . Remember . . .

NATALYA

It's all very well for you now . . . He's gone . . . Now we're both the same . . . *(Her voice breaks)*

VERA

Natalya Petrovna, you just said to me . . . these are your own words: instead of torturing each other, wouldn't it be better for us both to think how to get out of this situation, how to save ourselves? . . . We're saved now.

NATALYA

(Turning away from her almost with hatred) Oh . . .

VERA

I understand you, Natalya Petrovna . . . Don't worry . . . I won't burden you with my presence much longer. We can't live together.

NATALYA

(Wants to give her her hand and lets it drop on her knees) Why do you say that, Verochka . . . Do you want to leave me, too? Yes, you're right, we're saved now. It's all over . . . it's all fallen back into place . . .

VERA

(Coldly) Don't worry, Natalya Petrovna.

Vera looks at her silently. Islaev enters from the study.

ISLAEV

(Looking at Natalya Petrovna for a while, then to Vera in a low voice) Does she know he's leaving?

VERA

(In perplexity) Yes ... she does.

ISLAEV

(To himself) Why is he in such a rush ... *(Aloud)* Natasha ...

He takes her hand. She raises her head.

It's me, Natasha.

She tries to force a smile.

Are you unwell, darling? You ought to lie down, really ...

NATALYA

I'm quite well, Arkady ... It's nothing.

ISLAEV

You're pale, though ... Really, listen to me ... Get some rest.

NATALYA

Well, all right. *(She tries to get up and cannot)*

ISLAEV

(Helping her) There, you see ...

She leans on his arm.

Would you like me to go with you?

NATALYA

Oh, I'm not that weak yet! Let's go, Vera.

She heads for the study. Rakitin enters from the ballroom. Natalya Petrovna stops.

RAKITIN

Natalya Petrovna, I've come . . .

ISLAEV

(Interrupting him) Ah, Michel! Come here! *(Takes him aside and says in a low voice, vexedly)* Why did you just go and tell her straight away? I thought I asked you to wait! What was the hurry . . . I found her here so upset . . .

RAKITIN

(Amazed) I don't understand you.

ISLAEV

You told Natasha you're leaving . . .

RAKITIN

So you think that's why she's upset?

ISLAEV

Shh! She's looking at us. *(Aloud)* Aren't you going to your room, Natasha?

NATALYA

Yes . . . I'm going . . .

RAKITIN

Good-bye, Natalya Petrovna!

Natalya takes hold of the door handle—and does not answer.

ISLAEV

(Putting his hand on Rakitin's shoulder) You know, Natasha, this is one of the best of men . . .

NATALYA

(With sudden impulsiveness) Yes, I know, he's a wonderful man—
you're all wonderful . . . all, all . . . and yet . . .

*She suddenly covers her face with her hands, pushes the door with
her knee, and quickly exits. Vera exits after her. Islaev sits down
silently at the table, leaning his elbows on it.*

RAKITIN

*(Gazes at him for a while and shrugs with a bitter smile, then to him-
self)* What a situation! Nice, to say the least! Refreshing, even. And
what a farewell, after four years of love! Good, very good, serves
the babbler right. Thank God, it's all for the best. It was time to
break off these sick, consumptive relations. *(Aloud to Islaev)* Well,
good-bye, Arkady.

ISLAEV

(Raises his head. There are tears in his eyes) Good-bye, brother. It's
sort of . . . not so easy. I didn't expect it. Like a bolt from the blue.
Well, it will all come out right in the end. But thanks, thanks all the
same! You're a real friend!

RAKITIN

(To himself, through his teeth) This is too much! *(Abruptly)* Good-
bye.

*He is about to go to the ballroom . . . Shpigelsky comes running out
to him.*

SHPIGELSKY

What is it? They told me Natalya Petrovna's ill . . .

ISLAEV

(Getting up) Who told you?

SHPIGELSKY

The girl . . . the maid . . .

ISLAEV

It's nothing, doctor. I think it's better not to disturb Natasha just now . . .

SHPIGELSKY

Ah, well, excellent! *(To Rakitin)* I hear you're going to town?

RAKITIN

Yes. On business.

SHPIGELSKY

Ah, on business! . . .

Just then Anna Semyonovna, Lizaveta Bogdanovna, Kolya and Schaaf burst in all at once from the ballroom.

ANNA

What is it? What is it? What's wrong with Natasha?

KOLYA

What's wrong with mama? What's wrong with her?

ISLAEV

Nothing's wrong with her . . . I just saw her . . . What is all this?

ANNA

Good lord, Arkasha, we were told Natasha's ill . . .

ISLAEV

You shouldn't have believed it.

ANNA

Why are you angry, Arkasha? You can understand our concern . . .

ISLAEV

Of course . . . of course . . .

RAKITIN

Anyway, it's time for me to go.

ANNA

You're leaving?

RAKITIN

Yes . . . leaving.

ANNA

(To herself) Ah! Now I understand.

KOLYA

(To Islaev) Papa . . .

ISLAEV

What is it?

KOLYA

Why has Alexei Nikolaich gone away?

ISLAEV

Where has he gone?

KOLYA

I don't know . . . He kissed me, put his cap on, and left . . . It's time for my Russian lesson.

ISLAEV

He'll probably be back very soon . . . Or I could send for him.

RAKITIN

(In a low voice to Islaev) Don't send for him, Arkady. He won't come back.

Anna Semyonovna tries to eavesdrop. Shpigelsky exchanges whispers with Lizaveta Bogdanovna.

ISLAEV

What does that mean?

RAKITIN

He's gone.

ISLAEV

Gone? . . . Where?

RAKITIN

To Moscow.

ISLAEV

To Moscow! What, has everybody lost their minds today, or something?

RAKITIN

(Bending his head lower) Just between us . . . Verochka fell in love with him . . . Well, and so he, being an honorable man, decided to go away.

Islaev throws up his arms and sinks into the armchair.

Now you understand why . . .

ISLAEV

(Jumping up) Me? I understand nothing. My head's spinning. Nothing makes any sense! Everybody's scurrying in all directions like partridges, and it's all because they're honorable men . . . And all of them at once, on the same day . . .

ANNA

(Coming to him from the side) But what is it? Did you say Mr. Belyaev . . .

ISLAEV

(Shouts nervously) Never mind, mother, never mind! Mr. Schaaf, please give Kolya his lesson now instead of Mr. Belyaev. Please take him away.

SCHAAF

Fery goot, sir . . . *(Takes Kolya by the arm)*

KOLYA

But, papa . . .

ISLAEV

(Shouts) Out, out!

Schaaf exits with Kolya.

And you, Rakitin, I'll see you off . . . I'll have a horse saddled and wait for you at the dam . . . And in the meantime, mama, for God's sake don't disturb Natasha—and you, too, doctor . . . Matvei! Matvei!

Islaev exits hurriedly. Anna Semyonovna sits down with dignity and sorrow. Lizaveta Bogdanovna installs herself behind her. Anna Semyonovna raises her eyes to Heaven, as if wishing to be detached from everything happening around her.

SHPIGELSKY

(Furtively and slyly, to Rakitin) Well, Mikhail Alexandrych, can I give you a lift to the main road with my new little troika?

RAKITIN

Ah! . . . So you've already got it?

SHPIGELSKY

(Modestly) I had a talk with Vera Alexandrovna . . . Shall I give you a lift, sir?

RAKITIN

Why not! *(Bows to Anna Semyonovna)* Anna Semyonovna, I have the honor . . .

ANNA

(Still as majestically, not getting up) Good-bye, Mikhail Alexandrych . . . I wish you a pleasant journey . . .

RAKITIN

I humbly thank you. Lizaveta Bogdanovna . . .

He bows to her. She curtsies in response. He exits to the ballroom.

SHPIGELSKY

(Coming to kiss Anna Semyonovna's hand) Good-bye, madam . . .

ANNA

(Less majestically, but still sternly) Ah! You're leaving, too, doctor?

SHPIGELSKY

Yes, ma'am . . . Patients, you know. Besides, as you see, my presence here is not required.

As he makes his bows, he winks slyly at Lizaveta Bogdanovna, who responds with a smile.

Good-bye . . . *(Runs out after Rakitin)*

ANNA

(Waits until he leaves and, crossing her arms, turns slowly to Lizaveta Bogdanovna) What do you think of all this, my dear? Hm?

LIZAVETA

(Sighing) I don't know what to tell you, Anna Semyonovna.

ANNA

Have you heard? Belyaev has also left . . .

LIZAVETA

(Sighing again) Ah, Anna Semyonovna, I may not be staying here much longer myself . . . I'm leaving, too.

Anna Semyonovna looks at her with inexpressible amazement. Lizaveta Bogdanovna stands before her without raising her eyes.

CURTAIN

NOTES

1. *"Monte Cristo . . . haletant:"* "Monte Cristo straightened up, panting . . ." From *The Count of Monte Cristo*, by Alexandre Dumas (1802–1870).
2. *Ce que vous êtes pour moi*: "What you are for me." Russian aristocrats often spoke in French, especially in personal conversation.
3. *Wie befinden Sie sich?*: "how are you?"
4. *Ja, ja . . . zehr gut*: "Yes, yes, yes indeed, yes indeed, very good."
5. *Erlauben Sie . . . faule Leute*: "Permit me." "Come along." "Good morning, Mister Schaaf, good morning . . ." "Morning, morning, only not today, so all lazy people say."
6. *Gnädige Frau . . .* : "Madam."
7. *Es ist unerhört*: "This is outrageous."
8. *Mon enfant . . . le dîner*: "My child, you had better put on another dress for dinner."
9. Like Tatyana: Tatyana is the heroine of *Evgeny Onegin*, a novel in verse by Alexander Pushkin (1799–1837). She speaks these words near the end of the book (Chapter Eight, stanza XLVII),

confessing that she still loves Onegin as she dismisses him from her life.

10. *On n'entre pas . . . ne convient pas*: "One does not come into a room like that . . . It isn't proper."

11. Vera, *allez . . . monsieur*: "Vera, go on ahead with the gentleman."

12. *Beau ténébreux*: "Dark handsome stranger."

13. *Quelle tirade!*: "What a tirade!"

14. Paul de Kock . . . *Montfermeil*: Paul de Kock (1793–1871) was a prolific novelist of Parisian low life. He published *The Milkmaid of Montfermeil* in 1827.

15. *Souvent femme varie*: "Woman often changes."

16. Provincial Talleyrand: Prince Charles-Maurice de Talleyrand-Perigord (1754–1838), served as minister in French governments from Louis XIV on through the Revolution, Napoleon I, Louis XVIII, Charles X and Louis-Philippe, and represented France at the Congress of Vienna. A skillful diplomat and politician, he is sometimes portrayed as a schemer and even a traitor.

Production History

This translation of *A Month in the Country* premiered at Williamstown Theatre Festival (Jenny Gersten, Artistic Director; Stephen M. Kaus, Producer) in Williamstown, Massachusetts, on August 1, 2012. The director was Richard Nelson; the set design was by Takeshi Kata, the costume design was by Susan Hilferty, the lighting design was by Japhy Weideman, the sound design was by Drew Levy; the production stage manager was Eileen Ryan Kelly. The cast was:

ARKADY SERGEICH ISLAEV	Louis Cancelmi
NATALYA PETROVNA	Jessica Collins
KOLYA	Parker Bell-Devancy
VERA ALEXANDROVNA	Charlotte Bydwell
ANNA SEMYONOVNA ISLAEVA	Kate Kearney-Patch
LIZAVETA BOGDANOVNA	Elisabeth Waterston
MIKHAIL ALEXANDROVICH RAKITIN	Jeremy Strong
ALEXEI NIKOLAEVICH BELYAEV	Julian Cihi
AFANASY IVANOVICH BOLSHINTSOV	Paul Anthony McGrane
IGNATY ILYICH SHPIGELSKY	Sean Cullen

IVAN TURGENEV, one of the major Russian prose writers, a slightly older contemporary of Dostoevsky and Tolstoy, was born in the town of Orel, two hundred miles southwest of Moscow, in 1818, into a family of wealthy landowners. He attended the University of St. Petersburg, and from 1838 to 1841 studied philosophy and history at the University of Berlin. He wrote ten plays between 1843 and 1852, before turning definitively to prose fiction. Turgenev spent much of his adult life abroad, chiefly in France, where he died in the town of Bougival, near Paris, in 1883.

RICHARD NELSON's plays include the four-play series *The Apple Family: Scenes from Life in the Country* (*That Hopey Changey Thing, Sweet and Sad, Sorry* and *Regular Singing*), *Nikolai and the Others, Farewell to the Theatre, Conversations in Tusculum, How Shakespeare Won the West, Frank's Home, Rodney's Wife, Franny's Way, Madame Melville, Goodnight Children Everywhere, New England, The General from America, Misha's Party* (with Alexander Gelman), *Two Shakespearean Actors* and *Some Americans Abroad*. He has written the musicals *James Joyce's The Dead* (with Shaun Davey) and *My Life with Albertine* (with Ricky Ian Gordon), and the screenplays for the films *Hyde Park-on-Hudson* and *Ethan Frome*. He has received numerous awards, including a Tony (Best Book of a Musical for *James Joyce's The Dead*), an Olivier (Best Play for *Goodnight Children Everywhere*) and two New York Drama Critics' Circle Awards (*James Joyce's The Dead* and *The Apple Family*). He is the recipient of the PEN/Laura Pels Master Playwright Award, an Academy Award from the American

Academy of Arts and Letters; he is an Honorary Associate Artist of the Royal Shakespeare Company. He lives in upstate New York.

RICHARD PEVEAR was born in Boston, grew up on Long Island, attended Allegheny College (BA 1964) and the University of Virginia (MA 1965). After a stint as a college teacher, he moved to the Maine coast and eventually to New York City, where he worked as a freelance writer, editor and translator, and also as a cabinet-maker. He has published two collections of poetry, many essays and reviews, and some thirty books translated from French, Italian and Russian.

LARISSA VOLOKHONSKY was born in Leningrad, attended Leningrad State University and, on graduating, joined a scientific team whose work took her to the far east of Russia, to Kamchatka and Sakhalin Island. She emigrated to Israel in 1973, and to the United States in 1975, where she attended Yale Divinity School and St. Vladimir's Theological Seminary. Soon after settling in New York City, she married Richard Pevear, and a few years later they moved to France with their two children.

Together, Pevear and Volokhonsky have translated twenty books from the Russian, including works by Fyodor Dostoevsky, Leo Tolstoy, Mikhail Bulgakov, Anton Chekhov, Boris Pasternak and Nikolai Leskov. Their translation of Dostoevsky's *The Brothers Karamazov* received the PEN Translation Prize for 1991; their translation of Tolstoy's *Anna Karenina* was awarded the same prize in 2002; and in 2006 they were awarded the first Efim Etkind International Translation Prize by the European University of St. Petersburg.